SASKATCHEWAN
BOOK OF
Everything

Everything you wanted to know about
Saskatchewan and were going to ask anyway

Kelly-Anne Riess

MACINTYRE PURCELL PUBLISHING INC.

TO OUR READERS

Every effort has been made by authors and editors to ensure that the information enclosed in this book is accurate and up-to-date. We revise and update annually, however, many things can change after a book gets published. If you discover any out-of-date or incorrect information in the Nova Scotia Book of Musts, we would appreciate hearing from you via our website, **www.macintyrepurcell.com**.

We acknowledge the support of the Department of Canadian Heritage and the Nova Scotia Department of Tourism, Culture and Heritage in the development of writing and publishing in Canada.

MacIntyre Purcell Publishing Inc.
PO Box 1142
Lunenburg, Nova Scotia
B0J 2C0
(902) 640-2337
www.macintyrepurcell.com
info@macintyrepurcell.com

Cover photo courtesy of Ottmar Blerwagen
Photos: Pages: 8, 46, 78, 92, 128, 168, 184 Silas Polkinghorne
Photos: Pages: 36, 110, 198 Chad Coombs
Photos: Pages: 18, 64 Greg Johnson Photography
Cover and Design: Channel Communications Inc.

Printed and bound in Canada.

Library and Archives Canada Cataloguing in Publication
Riess, Kelly-Anne
Saskatchewan Book of Everything /
Kelly-Anne Riess
ISBN 0-9738063-9-7
Saskatchewan. 2. Saskatchewan--Miscellanea. I. Title.
FC3507.R53 2007   971.24
C2007-905134-0

Introduction

Of course one book could never really be about everything, but we hope the *Saskatchewan Book of Everything* comes close to capturing the essence of Saskatchewan and its people. Saskatchewan is a fascinating province and we could have filled volumes. In fact, our most difficult task by far was determining what to exclude.

As a born and raised Saskatchewanian who has lived in the province for most of my life, this book has been a reminder of why I continue to call Saskatchewan home. The province is a fabulously diverse place with a rich and interesting history. We have a lot to be proud of here. Sure, Saskatchewan may be the easiest Canadian province to draw, but Saskatchewan is rich in natural resources and has beautiful and varied scenery, which includes over 100,000 lakes and rivers. We can claim many talents, such as Joni Mitchell, Leslie Nielsen and Gordie Howe, as our own. We are home to the Saskatchewan Roughriders, the RCMP and the First Nations University of Canada. Saskatchewan is definitely a great place to live.

This book was very much a team effort. John MacIntyre and Martha Walls of MacIntyre Purcell Publishing were instrumental in conjuring up the concept of, and then producing, this book. A team of writers, myself included, worked tirelessly, combing through written material and surfing the web to bring together this massive collection of facts and stories. Any errors and omissions are our own.

I'd like to acknowledge and thank my fellow contributors, researchers and editors: Martha Walls, Silas Polkinghorne, Paul Spasoff, Erin Harde, Joan Cadham, Myrna Stark Leader, Carrie Anne MacIsaac, Lynn MacIntyre, Samantha Amara and Kelly Inglis.

The *Saskatchewan Book of Everything* team is richer for our newfound knowledge of Saskatchewan, and we hope our efforts will inform and entertain. We would like to extend a huge thank you to all those Saskatchewanians who shared their insight about the province for this book. The people here are, without a doubt, Saskatchewan's greatest attribute.

— Kelly-Anne Riess, for everyone who worked
on the *Saskatchewan Book of Everything*

Table of Contents

INTRODUCTION 3

SONG 7

TIMELINE 9
12,000 Before Present to Now . . . RCMP Establish Fort Walsh . . .
Tornado of 1912 . . . A Decade of Drought . . . Bill Waiser's Top Five
Saskatchewan Firsts . . . Snowbirds . . . Prince Albert Pulp Mill Closes . . .

ESSENTIALS 19
From the Origin of the Name to Population Trends . . . Melissa
Benett's Five Essential Saskatchewan Reads . . . Five Largest
Saskatchewan Cities . . . You Know You're From Saskatchewan When
. . . Higher Education . . .

SLANG 37
From Ag Bag Drag to Washboard, We Give You the Lowdown on
Saskatchewan Slang . . . Helen Mourre's Top Five Words to Describe
Saskatchewan . . .

THE NATURAL WORLD 47
Geographic Origins . . . The River . . . Scotty the T-Rex . . . Sharon
Butala's Five Saskatchewan Natural Wonders . . . Grey Owl . . . The
Great Gopher Derby . . . Hayley Wickenheiser's Top Five Favourite
Things About Growing Up Playing Hockey In Saskatchewan. . .
Largest Lakes and Longest Rivers . . . Athabasca Sand Dunes . . .

PLACE NAMES 65
Meanings and Origins of Select Place Names in the Province . . .
Sheila Coles' Top Reasons to Move to, and Settle In, Saskatchewan . .
. The Queen City . . . Paris of the Prairies . . .

WEATHER AND CLIMATE 79
Weather Winners . . . Weather Words . . . Pass the Shovel . . . Mud Season
. . . Regina Cyclone . . . Wind Power . . . Weather of Devastation . . .

CRIME AND PUNISHMENT 93
Crime Line . . . Big Muddy . . . Little Chicago . . . Wrong Man: The
David Milgaard Case . . . Carmen Harry Gives Up His Top Five Facts
About the RCMP . . . Neil Stonechild . . . To Serve and Protect . . .
The Musical Ride . . . .

CULTURE 111
From Guy Vanderhaeghe to Joni Mitchel to Corner Gas . . .Brad
Johner's Five Favourite Things About Saskatchewan. . . The Best
Summer Festivals . . . Shakespeare on the Saskatchewan . . .Hurry
Hard . . .Mr. Hockey and the Hall of Fame . . . Ankle Bones . . .

ECONOMY 129
From GDP to Taxes . . . Average Wages . . . Paul Martin's Five Best
Things About Doing Business In Saskatchewan. . . King of Potash . . .
Who Makes What . . . The Hill Family . . . Small Business. . . Five
Largest Employers . . . Self Employment . . . Infrastructure . . . Gas and
Oil . . . Agribusiness

POLITICS 151
Governance Before Government . . . Tommy Douglas: Father of
Medicare . . . Premiers and Their Occupations . . . Women in Politics
. . . The Saskatchewan Party . . . Lorne Calvert's Five Favourite
Things About Saskatchewan . . .

THEN AND NOW 169
Bill Brennan's Top Five People in Saskatchewan History . . . All the Live
Long Day . . . Sigga Arnason's Favourite Things About Growing Up in
Saskatchewan . . . Regina Riot . . . Dr. Stuart Houston's Top Five
Saskatchewan Heathcare Firsts . . . Saskatchewan Roughriders . . .

FIRST PEOPLE 185
In the Beginning . . . Chief Poundmaker . . . Reserves . . . Simon
Moccasin's Five Reactions and Consequences if the Infamous "60's Scoop"
. . . Sundance . . . Joan Beatty . . . Buffy Sainte-Marie . . . Treaties . . .

GO AHEAD, TAKE FIVE MORE 199
Wayne Mantkya's Top Moments Reporting News in Saskatchewan . . .
Chef Moe Mathieu's Favourite Dishes . . . Kevin Hursh Tells His Five
Most Important Farm Innovations . . . Amy Jo Ehman's Favourite
Saskatchewan Cookbooks . . . Linda Matthew's Favourite Fruit Crops
Grown in Saskatchewan . . . Noelle Chorney's Favourite Eating Patios
. . . Gerry Klein on Saskatchewan Innovations . . . Derek Turner's Top
Five Free Things to Do

SASKATCHEWAN SONG

Stan Garchinski's entertainment career began with a family dance band called the Cavaliers in Naicam, Saskatchewan. In 1983 he toured with Up With People and was a feature vocalist on their live album. In 1989 Garchinski released a solo album *Small Town Living* and appeared on national television during the 1995 half-time show for the Grey Cup.

As a singer-songwriter, Garchinski has written and recorded several songs, including "We Sing Saskatchewan", Saskatchewan's 90th anniversary theme song. Since 1990, Garchinski has been performing with the Hot Tamales, a Saskatoon-based party band. In addition to playing with the Hot Tamales, Garchinski is a guitarist and vocalist with The Spirit of the Cross, a contemporary Christian group. In 2005, Garchinski penned "Saskatchewan, We Love This Place!" which was selected as the official theme song for the province's 100th birthday. He followed up by releasing a new solo album, *In My Chevrolet*, in 2006.

SASKATCHEWAN, WE LOVE THIS PLACE!

I have shared your laughter - I have shared your tears
I have watched you grow for a hundred years
I have walked your cities - I have breathed your country air
I love this place, I love it here

CHORUS
We are many and we are one
Lift your voice and sing Saskatchewan
We are many and we are one
Cause we love this place Saskatchewan

I have seen your strength and I have felt your love
With hearts as big as the skies above
I have seen your rivers run fast and run strong
I love this place - its where I belong

CHORUS

One hundred years we celebrate with joy
We celebrate with joy a hundred years
One hundred years we celebrate with joy
We celebrate with joy one hundred years

CHORUS

CHORUS

Saskatchewan:

A Timeline

12,000 Before Present: The Wisconsin Glacier recedes.

11,000 Before Present: First People from various nations live in the area now known as Saskatchewan.

1690: The first European, Henry Kelsey of the Hudson's Bay Company (HBC), comes to buy furs from the First People.

1774: Samuel Hearne builds a HBC fur trading post at Cumberland House, the company's first inland post and the first permanent settlement in the area now known as Saskatchewan.

1870: Canada pays the HBC £300,000 sterling, about $1,460,000 in 1870 dollars, for the three million hectare Rupert's Land and the Northwestern Territory.

1871: The first in a series of treaties are signed between First People and the Canadian government.

1872: Canada's Dominion Lands Act encourages settlement with cheap land. Male heads of household over age 21 pay a $10 registration fee and in return are given a quarter section (160 acres or 65 hectares).

1875: The Royal Canadian Mounted Police (RCMP) establishes Fort Walsh in the Southwest.

1883: The Métis, a group of people of mixed European (usually French) and Aboriginal descent, are dissatisfied with Ottawa's administration of the North West. Led by Louis Riel, they demand self-government.

1885: After months of tension, frustrated Métis rebel against federal officials. A series of skirmishes end with a final four-day showdown at Batoche. Riel is captured, charged with high treason and is hanged in Regina on November 16, 1885.

1891: Fire destroys 17 businesses and a church in Moose Jaw. The blaze inspires new town regulations requiring buildings be made of brick or stone.

1905: Saskatchewan enters Confederation. Former owner-editor of the *Regina Leader*, 37-year old Liberal Thomas Walter Scott, is named premier.

1906: Regina becomes the provincial capital.

They Said It

"I am more convinced every day that without a single exception I did right. And I have always believed that. The time will come when the people of Canada will see and acknowledge it."

– Louis Riel

Louis Riel and the Northwest Rebellion

In 1884, the Métis of the Northwest Territories in what is now Saskatchewan, were starving. The bison upon which they depended were virtually extinct and the transition to farming proved difficult. Meanwhile, they were outraged as Canadian Pacific Railway laid tracks through Métis territory without regard to their land title. Frustrated and impoverished, the desperate Métis called on Louis Riel who had led the Métis fight at Red River a decade and a half earlier.

Believing he'd been chosen by God to lead his people, Riel returned from the United States and organized a series of public meetings. These discussions resulted in the 1885 "Revolutionary Bill of Rights" asserting Métis rights of possession to their farms.

On March 18 and 19, the Métis formed a provisional government based at Batoche. Riel was president, Gabriel Dumont, military commander. The provisional government flexed muscle by taking prisoners. Expecting police retaliation, the Métis amassed forces at Duck Lake, midway between Batoche and Fort Carlton.

On March 26, the Northwest Mounted Police, aided by citizen volunteers, traveled to Duck Lake. En route they were met by the the Métis. A short battle ensued. Before government forces retreated to Fort Carlton, nine volunteers, three police and six Métis were dead.

Ottawa, alarmed by escalating violence, sent in reinforcements. On April 12, the Métis initiated the first of a series of battles when they attacked Canadian recruits at Fish Creek. A second battle followed at Cut Knife Hill on May 1. Then, on May 9 came the bloodiest skirmish. Canadian forces began a three-day siege at Batoche. The Métis were defeated and the North West Rebellion came to an end.

Days later, Riel surrendered. Charged with treason, he stood trial in Regina. Riel's defense argued that his religious and political delusions prevented him from comprehending the nature of his offense. Riel's own testimony, however, was as impassioned as it was cogent. He was no madman. Riel was found guilty and was hanged in Regina on November 16, 1885.

1906: Treaty Ten sees Ottawa and First People of northern Saskatchewan negotiate the province's final numbered treaty.

1907: The University of Saskatchewan is created.

1908: Saskatchewan gets a provincial telephone system.

1911: Rosthern farmer Seager Wheeler wins the first of five world wheat championships with Marquis wheat, an early maturing variety first tested at the experimental farm in Indian Head, Saskatchewan.

1911: Farmers form the Saskatchewan Co-operative Elevator Company.

1912: An opulent new Legislature, with a price tag of $1.8 million, opens in Regina.

1912: A tornado hits Regina leaving 28 dead, thousands homeless, and destroys hundreds of buildings.

1914: The Juniata Co-operative Association forms under Saskatchewan's new co-operative legislation. Soon, there are 113 co-operatives in the province.

1914: The rural municipality of Sarnia is the first in North America to use its own money to hire a doctor.

Did you know...

that on 'Gopher Day,' May 1, 1917, school children from almost 1,000 Saskatchewan schools competed to destroy the greatest number of gophers? Regarded as destructive agricultural pests, the children killed over half a million gophers in the process, saving an estimated $385,000 in grain.

Take 5 BILL WAISER'S TOP FIVE SASKATCHEWAN FIRSTS

University of Saskatchewan history professor Bill Waiser is author of the award-winning, *Saskatchewan: A New History*.

1. On March 14, 1923, Regina's CKCK made broadcasting history when Pete Parker called the play-by-play between the Capitals and the visiting Edmonton Eskimos of the Western Canada professional hockey league. Foster Hewitt made his radio debut from Toronto's Maple Leaf Gardens nine days later.

2. In 1927, Christina Riepsamen, a Regina guide leader, came up with a simple but novel way to raise money for uniforms and camping equipment for her group. She baked cookies in her home, packaged them in brown paper bags, and then asked her girls to sell them for ten cents a dozen to friends and neighbours. The idea was an instant success and quickly spread to other groups. In 1929, the sale of cookies became an official Girl Guide activity.

3. The Co-operative Commonwealth Federation, led by Baptist minister Tommy Douglas, formed the first socialist government in North America when it was elected by a landslide in June 1944. The Douglas government introduced a number of firsts – especially in the health field.

4. The first automated teller machine in Canada was set up by the Sherwood Credit Union in Regina. Saskatchewan also introduced the first debit cards and debit card transaction in North America.

5. The First Nations University of Canada, formerly known as the Saskatchewan Indian Federated College, was the first Indian-controlled post-secondary educational institution in Canada when it opened its doors in 1975.

1916: Saskatchewan begins eight years of legislated prohibition against alcohol.

1916: Only Saskatchewan women who are British subjects can vote in municipal and provincial elections.

1920: Regina flies high with four Canadian aviation firsts – Roland Groome gets the first commercial pilot's license, Robert McCombie receives the first air engineer's certificate, the province's first licensed airport is built, and the first commercial airplane is licensed.

1924: The Saskatchewan Wheat Pool forms. It will become the largest co-operative marketing organization in the world.

1928: Prince Albert National Park, the first in Saskatchewan, opens north of Saskatoon. It later becomes the home of famed conservationist Grey Owl.

1929: Saskatchewan feels the effects of the Great Depression and the beginning of a decade of drought.

1929: The provincial Saskatchewan Power Commission is established.

1931: Three coal miners die in Estevan when striking miners, who come to town to protest low wages and poor living conditions, clash with police.

1932: Provincial income tax is instituted, a "temporary" plan to rescue Saskatchewan from the Great Depression.

Did you know...

that in 2001, Saskatchewan became the first place in North America to ban the promotion and display of tobacco products in retail stores to which children have access? On January 1, 2005, all public places in Saskatchewan went smoke-free.

1932: A new Saskatchewan-based national political party, the Saskatchewan Farmer-Labour party, is formed. It later becomes the Saskatchewan Co-operative Commonwealth Federation.

1933: The Co-operative Commonwealth Federation adopts the Regina Manifesto calling for an end to capitalism and for the nationalization of railways, banks, public utilities and other services.

1934: The first natural gas well begins commercial production near Lloydminster. Eleven years later the city is home to the province's first commercial oil well.

1935: A riot erupts in downtown Regina between out-of-work men and police. One worker and one police officer die in the fray.

1935: Regina takes to the world stage by opening the first ever co-operative oil refinery.

1940: Construction begins on 14 British Commonwealth Air Training Plan bases.

1944: Saskatchewanians elect the Co-operative Commonwealth Federation and T.C. (Tommy) Douglas becomes premier.

1947: Saskatchewan residents pay five dollars each (or $30 per family) to have universal hospital insurance, a Canadian first.

1951: In London, Ontario and Saskatoon, two cancer patients are treated with radiation (The Cobalt Bomb), revolutionizing cancer treatment around the world.

1952: Saskatchewan's first uranium mine opens.

1957: Progressive Conservative John G. Diefenbaker, a lawyer in Prince Albert and Wakaw, becomes Prime Minister.

1962: Saskatchewan implements Medicare. The tax-funded system provides medical care to all residents and becomes the model for the national program.

1966: After eight unsuccessful attempts, the Saskatchewan Roughriders defeat the Ottawa Rough Riders in the Grey Cup Championship.

1971: North America's future largest annual livestock show, the Canadian Western Agribition, begins in Regina.

1971: The Saskatchewan Homecoming Air Show hosts the first public appearance of Moose Jaw's air acrobatic team, the Snowbirds.

1981: The government agreed to establish the province's second national park, Grasslands, south of Swift Current.

1982: Saskatchewan First Nation Chiefs form the Federation of Saskatchewan Indian Nations, Canada's first Indian legislative assembly. The same year, more than 20,000 people attend the World Assembly of First Nations in Regina.

1989: The Roughriders win the 77th Grey Cup, defeating the Hamilton Tiger-Cats 43-40.

1991: Big Bert, the world's most complete Telorhinus skeleton, a prehistoric crocodile, is found on the bank of the Carrot River. Three years later, one of the most complete T-Rex skeletons, Scotty, is excavated near Eastend.

1992: Wauskewin Heritage Park, home to over 6,000 years of northern plains First Nations cultural interpretations, opens near Saskatoon.

2004: Canada's only light source synchrotron opens in Saskatoon. The synchrotron uses a very bright light to help researchers determine what materials are made of.

2005: Saskatchewan celebrates its centennial.

2006: British Columbian Kyle MacDonald makes headlines when, though a series of eBay trades, he turns a single red paper clip into a house in Kipling.

2006: The Prince Albert Pulp Mill, the province's largest industrial employer when it was built in 1968, closes and puts 690 people out of work.

2007: Saskatchewan's premier travels to Calgary to lure people to the province by praising Saskatchewan as the land of affordable housing and short commutes. Saskatchewan continues to lose people to other Western provinces, but records a population increase for the first time since 1995.

2010: Saskatchewan athletes earn an impressive 11 medals in total (nine of them gold) at the 2010 Vancouver Olympics. Medal recipients include: Corinne Bartel, silver in women's curling • Ryan Getzlaf, gold in men's ice hockey • Ben Hebert, gold in men's curling • Gina Kingsbury, gold in women's ice hockey • Lucas Makowsky, gold in speed skating team pursuit • Patrick Marleau, gold in men's ice hockey • Meaghan Mikkelson, gold in women's ice hockey • Brenden Morrow, gold in men's ice hockey • Lyndon Rush, bronze in men's bobsleigh • Colleen Sostorics, gold in women's ice hockey • Hayley Wickenheiser, gold in women's ice hockey.

2010: Canpotex Limited, the offshore marketing company of Saskatchewan's potash producers, reaches a new agreement with Sinofert Holdings Limited of China to sell its potash to China at $576 US per tonne, a $400 per tonne increase over the 2007 price.

2011: Canada rejects BHP Billiton's $39bn bid for PotashCorp, the Saskatchewan-based fertilizer producer. Ottawa invokes rarely used foreign investment review law.

2012: The province is experiencing an unprecedented boom, replete with labour shortages and buoyant optimism. After leading the nation in economic growth in 2011, Saskatchewan will do so again 2012.

Essentials

Origin of the Name: From the Plains Cree word, "kisiskatchewan," meaning "the river that flows swiftly."

Provincial Capital: Regina

License Plate: "Land of Living Skies" was added to the Saskatchewan license plate in 1998.

Motto: *Multis E Gentibus Vires*, "From Many Peoples Strength."

Coat of Arms: Granted in 1986, the provincial Coat of Arms features a crest of a beaver and a crown that sits above the shield which is supported by a lion and a deer. The shield boasts a royal lion and three gold wheat sheaves, symbolizing Saskatchewan's agriculture, below which is a banner with the provincial motto. Western red lilies, Saskatchewan's floral emblem, appear on the base.

Provincial Flag: Adopted in 1969, Saskatchewan's official flag features the provincial shield of arms along with the floral emblem, the western red lily. The flag's upper half is green, representing

Saskatchewan's northern forests. The lower half is gold, symbolizing the southern grain areas.

Provincial Flower: In 1941, the western red lily or *Lilium philadelphicum*, was chosen as the provincial flower. This protected species, which sports flaming red blossoms, grows in moist meadows and semi-wooded areas.

Take 5 — MELISSA BENNETT'S TOP FIVE BOOKS ABOUT SASKATCHEWAN

Born and raised in Regina, Melissa Bennett was has worked for sixteen years in the library sector in Saskatchewan. She is currently Legislative Librarian in the Saskatchewan Legislative Library. Additional significant Saskatchewan books can be found at www.bookawards.sk.ca and local libraries www.mylibrary.sk.ca.

1. *Atlas of Saskatchewan* edited by Ka-iu Fung. Saskatoon: University of Saskatchewan, 1999 (Millenium Edition). The Atlas of Saskatchewan "portrays the province's heritage and history, physical environment, wildlife, natural resources, population, native peoples, economic activities and major cities, in individual themes and in their interrelations and interactions over space and times." A top 5 list of books about Saskatchewan would not be complete without this momentous work.

2. *Ahtahkakoop: The Epic Account of a Plains Cree Head Chief, His People, and Their Struggle for Survival 1816-1896* by Deanna Christensen. Shell Lake: Ahtahkakoop Publishing, 2000. This 800 page volume, which won a Saskatchewan Book Award, is a significant achievement in the recording of the history and culture of Aboriginal people in Saskatchewan. Its development involved thirteen years of close collaboration between the author and Ahtahkatoop's descendents. It is a captivating story supported by extensive oral histories and research.

Provincial Bird: The sharp-tailed grouse, or *Tympanuchus phasianellus*, a popular game bird, was named the provincial bird in 1945.

Provincial Tree: The White Birch (or Paper Birch), *Betula papyrifera*, was adopted as the official tree in 1988. Found across the northern three-quarters of the province, this hardwood is typically used for lumber, plywood, veneer and fuel.

3. *The Encyclopedia of Saskatchewan: A Living Legacy*. Regina: Canadian Plains Research Centre, University of Regina, 2005. The Encyclopedia of Saskatchewan is a towering collective achievement. Its production involved contributions from over 700 individuals and the collaboration of a significant number of Saskatchewan organizations. It is an essential Saskatchewan reference book.

4. *Saskatchewan Premiers of the Twentieth Century* edited by Gordon L. Barnhart. Regina: Canadian Plains Research Centre, 2004. This collection of biographies (a chapter for each premier) illuminates the lives, times, responsibilities and accomplishments of Saskatchewan's premiers. The various authors have crafted insightful and readable histories that highlight the complexity and challenge of navigating the political realm and leading a province.

5. *Saskatchewan: A New History by Bill Waiser* (Calgary: Fifth House Ltd., 2005). Bill Waiser, a historian at the University of Saskatchewan and a prolific author, has delivered a history of Saskatchewan to the present day that is both a serious historical reference work and an enjoyable read.

Take 5 FIVE LARGEST SASKATCHEWAN CITIES (POPULATION)

1. **Saskatoon** (234,200)
2. **Regina** (200,902)
3. **Prince Albert** (35,629)
4. **Moose Jaw** (32,132)
5. **Yorkton** (15,038)

Provincial Grass: In 2001, needle-and-thread grass, or *Hesperostipa comata*, was designated Saskatchewan's official grass. The grass gets its name from the shape of its seeds, which are sharply pointed and have long, twisted, thread-like fibres.

Provincial Tartan: The Saskatchewan provincial tartan was registered with the Court of Lord Lyon King of Arms in Scotland in 1961. It has seven colours: gold, brown, green, red, yellow, white and black.

Provincial Mineral: Sylvite (potash) is Saskatchewan's official mineral.

Provincial Animal: In 2001 Saskatchewan designated the white-tailed deer, or *Odocoileus virginianus*, its official animal. The deer's name comes from the white underside of the tail, which is raised like a flag when the deer runs or is frightened.

Provincial Sport: Curling was named Saskatchewan's official sport in 2001.

Did you know...

that Saskatchewan is the only province with entirely man-made boundaries?

They Said It

> *"There is no privacy, because your neighbour, even though he be ten miles off, can from his window observe you hanging out your clothes in your garden, or hoeing your turnips, and can almost see what you are having for dinner."*
> **– Observance of Harry Graham, who passed through Regina on his way to the Klondike goldfields in 1900.**

Time Zone: Central Standard Time, except for Lloydminster, a town which straddles the Saskatchewan-Alberta border and uses Mountain Time. Apart from the communities of Denare Beach and Creighton, Saskatchewan does not use Daylight Saving Time.

Statutory Holidays: Saskatchewan celebrated Family Day for the first time on February 19, 2007. The province, along with the Northwest Territories, has 10 statutory holidays – more than any province or territory in Canada. They are: New Year's Day, Family Day, Good Friday, Victoria Day, Canada Day, Saskatchewan Day (1st Monday in August), Labour Day, Thanksgiving Day, Remembrance Day, and Christmas Day.

Location: Situated in the heart of North America, to the east and west of Saskatchewan are the Canadian provinces of Manitoba and Alberta. To the south it borders the American states of Montana and North Dakota. To the north are Canada's North West Territories and Nunavut.

Nickname: Land of Living Skies

They Said It

> *"Saskatchewan, hard to spell, easy to draw."*
> **– A popular, very true, T-shirt slogan.**

YOU KNOW YOU'RE FROM

- You know what a Saskatchewanian is. And you can spell it.
- Throwing rocks at houses doesn't get you in trouble with the law, but it does help your curling team.
- You can't understand why those American television networks never settle on a schedule, instead of shifting all their programs back and forth an hour every spring and fall.
- You make your chili the same way everyone else does . . . wait, doesn't everyone use bison meat?
- You catch yourself "getting down" to the radio jingles for post-emergent broad-leaf weed control.
- You have a ball cap to match every shirt you own, but you insist on wearing only one so the others don't get dirty.
- When the bank teller asks for some form of identification, you point to the arm patch on your slow-pitch jacket.
- You've read *Who Has Seen the Wind* a million times, and counting.
- Your pronunciation of "Saskatchewan" is nearly monosyllabic: "Skatchw'n."
- You are familiar with the sight of a running car sitting in the store parking with no one in it at any given time of the year.
- You think of Winnipeg as being "back east."
- Your cupboards boast four spices: salt, pepper, ketchup and cheese whiz.
- You know what a prairie oyster is and have a recipe for them.
- You've witnessed someone stick his/her tongue to a metal fence in the winter.
- For some inexplicable reason, you have stuck your tongue to a metal fence.
- You've purchased a "to go" drink from a local bar.
- You've thrown an extension cord out your third floor apartment window to plug in your car.
- You consider gopher road kill as the first sign of spring.
- You carry a scarf, toque and mittens with you until mid-May, "just in case."
- Your dog runs away and you can still see him two days later.
- You call it a bunnyhug, and not a hoodie.
- Dinner is at noon, not in the evening. The evening meal is supper.
- You can't skip class and go to the store because every person downtown knows you and your parents, and they know you should be in school.

SASKATCHEWAN WHEN...

- You never realized you had a fear of heights until the day you made the mistake of peering down an open well.
- You can perfectly understand the mute Gainer.
- Your bumper sticker reads: "My other car is a John Deere."
- Your definition of "rush hour" is five minutes spent waiting through two stoplights on the way home from work.
- You've visited a small town heritage museum housed in a converted grain elevator.
- Driving in the winter is often a matter of staying between the fence posts.
- You can recite from memory the names of the towns, in order, along the highway from Regina to Saskatoon.
- Your town is very proudly known as the home of the world's largest moose/teapot/tomahawk, etc.
- You really can taste the difference between Alberta and Saskatchewan beef.
- You get teary eyed when you return from the big city and spy a grain elevator silhouette on the horizon.
- You laugh when you hear about "snowstorms" in Vancouver and Victoria.
- You watch "Corner Gas" because it reminds you of home.
- You see no compelling reason to own a rain jacket.
- Every winter you complain about your town's snow removal strategy, and every summer you complain about its street repair schedule.
- When you visit another province and someone asks if you know his friend Susan in Saskatoon, it turns out you actually do.
- You know that the true beauty of a place isn't found on the landscape – it's in the sky.
- You moved to Alberta to find a job after graduation, but you can't wait to move back.
- Losing sight of the horizon, for even a few seconds, disorients you for the rest of the day.
- You sort your laundry into three loads: greens, whites and green-and-whites.
- You know how to hurry hard.
- You can tell when it's almost Christmas because stores stay open late TWO nights a week rather than one.

Saskatchewan is home to 13 cities: Estevan, Humboldt, Lloydminster, Melfort, Melville, Moose Jaw, North Battleford, Prince Albert, Regina, Saskatoon, Swift Current, Weyburn, Yorkton

Largest City: Saskatoon, Population 234,200

Capital City: Regina

System of measurement: Metric

Voting age: 18

SISTER CITIES

On August 10, 1987, the city of Regina twinned with the city of Jinan, Province of Shandong, People's Republic of China. The twinning was intended to foster exchanges and co-operation in economy, trade, science and technology, culture, education and city administration. Jinan (pop. five million) is located 350 km south of China's capital, Beijing, and covers an area of 8,227 km^2.

POPULATION BREAKDOWN

Total Population	1,063,535
Male	49.7 percent
Female	50.3 percent
Rural	64 percent
Urban	36 percent

Source: Statistics Canada.

Did you know...

that the city of Estevan in southeast Saskatchewan is Canada's sunshine capital, averaging 2,540 sunshine-filled hours each year?

POPULATION DENSITY (PEOPLE/KM²)

Saskatchewan	1.7
Alberta	4.6
Ontario	12.6
Nova Scotia	17.8
Toronto	3,939
New York City	10,194
Tokyo	13,416

Source: aapinfoweb.

FARMS

- Number of farm families in 1996: 45,585
- Number of farm families in 2001: 38,605

Source: Statistics Canada.

POPULATION IN PERSPECTIVE

The year 2007 marked the first time Saskatchewan's population has topped one million since July 1, 2001, and in 2010 it has the second highest annual growth rate in the country. Alberta, which is similar in area, boasts a population of 3,632,483— more than three times that of Saskatchewan.

If Saskatchewan were an American state it would come in 43rd in terms of population, with slightly fewer residents than Rhode Island's 1,067,610 and slightly more residents than Montana's 944,632.

Source: Statistics Canada.

Did you know...

that while Lloydminster has a total population of 24,028, only 8,118 of its residents live in Saskatchewan? The city straddles the Alberta-Saskatchewan border and shares its citizens with Alberta. As a result, the community is just the 11th largest municipality in Saskatchewan.

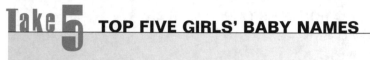

Take 5 TOP FIVE GIRLS' BABY NAMES

1. Madison
2. Emma
3. Olivia
4. Hailey
5. Ava

CRADLE TO GRAVE

Births   12,031
Deaths   9,250

Source: Statistics Canada.

MARRIAGE

- Number of marriages: 4,977
- Rate of marriage in Saskatchewan (per 1,000 population): 5.0
- Marriage rate in Nunavut, Canada's lowest: 2.3
- Marriage rate in Prince Edward Island, Canada's highest: 6.0
- National marriage rate: 4.7
- Age of groom at first marriage: 29.3
- Age of bride at first marriage: 27.0

Source: Statistics Canada.

Did you know...

that Saskatchewan's total road surface would circle the equator four times?

Take 5 — TOP FIVE BOYS' BABY NAMES

1. **Ethan**
2. **Joshua**
3. **Matthew**
4. **Carter**
5. **Logan**

D-I-V-O-R-C-E

- The divorce rate (per 100 marriages) in Saskatchewan: 29
- The divorce rate in Quebec, the highest: 49.7
- The divorce rate in Prince Edward Island, the lowest: 27.3
- The divorce rate nationally: 38.3

Source: Statistics Canada.

FAMILY STRUCTURE

- Number of all families (married and common law, single parent): 265,620
- Families with children: 61.1%
- Families without children: 38.9%
- Single parent (male): 3.0%
- Single parent (female): 12.9%

Source: Statistics Canada.

They Said It

> "Whether in rural settings, towns or cities, we have met citizens of Saskatchewan, of many diverse backgrounds, who are united in their desire to continue to build a society that will remain the envy of the world."
>
> – Queen Elizabeth II

They Said It

RELIGIOUS AFFILIATION

Protestant	46.6%
Catholic	31.7%
None	15.7%
Other Christian	2.8%
Christian Orthodox	1.5%
Buddhist	0.3%
Muslim	0.2%
Hindu	0.1%
Jewish	0.1%
Eastern religions	0.1%
Sikh	0.1%
Other religions	0.7%

Source: Statistics Canada.

Did you know...

that in 1998, Saskatoon's Catriona LeMay Doan won Canada's first gold medal in women's speed skating? Three years later she was named Canadian Female Athlete of the Year.

LANGUAGES (PERCENTAGE OF PEOPLE WHO CAN SPEAK)

English	85.8%
German	3.4%
Cree	2.3%
Ukrainian	2.10%
French	1.9%
Chinese	0.6%
Polish	0.3%
Spanish	0.2%
Dutch	0.2%
Tagalog	0.2%
Vietnamese	0.1%
Arabic	0.1%
Greek	0.1%
Italian	0.1%
Punjabi	0.05%
Portuguese	0.04%
Other	2.5%

- Saskatchewan residents who speak more than one language: 9,650
- English and French 1,375
- English and non-official language 7,910
- French and non-official language 255
- English, French and non-official language 115

Source: Statistics Canada.

Did you know...

that curling was once called the "roaring game" because of the thunderous noise made by corn brooms used to sweep rocks down the ice?

FOOTBALL

Although they play in the Canadian Football League's (CFL) smallest market, the Saskatchewan Roughriders have the distinction of being the league's most loved team. On October 14, 1995, 55,438 fans crammed into Regina's Taylor Field – quite a feat considering it has a capacity of just 27,732 – to watch the Roughriders beat Calgary 25 to 23. Rider Pride makes every home game a province-wide celebration.

The Roughriders have won the Grey Cup three times – 1966, 1989, and 2007 though they appeared in the final in 2009 and 2010.

HOCKEY

The Saskatchewan Junior Hockey League has 12 teams. The junior teams have won the Royal Bank Cup twice. The Humboldt Broncos won in 2003 and the Weyburn Red Wings won in 2005.

SCHOOLS AND STUDENTS
- Total number of schools   747
- Total number of students   163,311
- Number of public schools   616
- Public school enrollment   127,028
- Number of separate schools   118
- Separate schools enrollment   35,170
- Number of francophone schools   13
- Francophone schools enrollment   1,113

Source: Government of Saskatchewan.

HIGHER EDUCATION

Saskatchewan has two provincial universities: the University of Saskatchewan (U of S) in Saskatoon and the University of Regina (U of R) in Regina. Both offer internationally recognized Bachelor's, Master's and Doctoral degree programs in addition to other diploma and certificate programs.

The University of Saskatchewan had 15,000 full-time students, 4,000 part-time students, and 8,000 extension students and receives $115 million a year in research funding.

Since achieving independence from the University of Saskatchewan in 1974, the University of Regina has grown to nine faculties and 23 departments. Student enrollment exceeds 12,500 full- and part-time students with a faculty and staff of about 1,200.

The Saskatchewan Indian Federated College was created in 1976 by agreement between the Federation of Saskatchewan Indian Nations and the University of Regina and serves the academic, cultural and spiritual needs of First Nation students. In 2003, the First Nations University of Canada opened its doors at the U of R. It offers programs in ten academic departments and in three communities: Regina, Saskatoon and Prince Albert.

The Saskatchewan Institute of Applied Science and Technology (SIAST) provides has more than 200 certificate and diploma programs at campuses in Moose Jaw, Prince Albert, Regina and Saskatoon.

Source: SaskNetWork.

Did you know...

that Saskatchewan was the first province in Canada to adopt an air ambulance service?

HEALTH CARE, BY THE NUMBERS
- Number of physicians in Saskatchewan: 1,545
- Number of nurses: 9,000+
- Number of dentists: 366

Source: Saskatchewan Registered Nurses Association; Canadian Institute for Health Information; Firstmark.

HOSPITALS
In addition to the major hospitals of Regina and Saskatoon, 87 communities around the province have smaller regional hospitals.

Saskatoon
St. Paul's Hospital is an acute care teaching facility serving Saskatoon and Northern Saskatchewan.

The Royal University hospital houses the province's main trauma center, maternal and child services, neurosurgery and cardiovascular surgery.

Saskatoon City Hospital is home to the SaskTel MRI Suite. It is also one of the few acute care hospitals in Canada to house a research centre — the Cameco MS Neuroscience Research Centre.

Regina
The Regina General Hospital houses Canada's first factory-delivered, eight-slice Computed Tomography (CT) and houses a new Magnetic Resonance Imaging machine(MRI).

The Pasqua Hospital is Regina's second main hospital.

Source: Government of Saskatchewan; Hospitals of Regina.

RURAL HEALTH CARE

Rural Saskatchewanians can see medical specialists in their home communities through the two-way video communication of Telehealth Saskatchewan's Clinical Services. The province has 26 tele-health network sites and a 24 hour health information line which field more than 85,000 calls every year.

Source: Government of Saskatchewan.

Weblinks

Encyclopedia of Saskatchewan

http://esask.uregina.ca/the_story.html

This user-friendly website provides a wealth of information on Saskatchewan, from Aberdeen to Zooplankton.

Virtual Saskatchewan

http://www.virtualsk.com/current_issue/ought3.html

Virtual Saskatchewan is an on-line magazine with information on all things Saskatchewan, all just the click of a mouse away!

Celebrating Saskatchewan's Heritage

http://olc.spsd.sk.ca/de/saskatchewan100/index.html

This website, created by Saskatoon Public Schools, Online Learning Centre in partnership with the Western Development Museum, provides movies, audio files and information on a variety of Saskatchewan topics.

Saskatchewan Slang:
A Dictionary of Saskatchewan English

The language of a place defines it. It describes local phenomena and events, outlines a place's history and, most importantly, it binds people in a bond of shared understanding. Saskatchewan, like so many places, has a distinct dialect that unites its people with a common identity.

Acre: How the majority of Saskatchewanians refer to a measure of land even though the country changed to hectares over two decades ago.

Agro: A student of Agriculture at the University of Saskatchewan.

Ag Bag Drag: An annual event hosted by the Agriculture Student's Association at the University of Saskatchewan. This is one big party.

Back forty: A piece of land (technically 40 acres) or a field that is away from the home on a farm, or a remote location.

Back, outside or summer kitchen: A farm house's second kitchen. Located outside the main house, this is where cooking and canning was done during the very hot summer to keep the heat out of the house.

Badlands: A barren and desert-like area in Southwestern Saskatchewan.

Bannock: Unleavened bread made using flour, water and sometimes, lard.

Bee: A cooperative work session where neighbours and family come together to complete a project. In Saskatchewan bees are common – and are used for every task from barn-raising to perogy-making.

Bin: A place to store grain. No particular storage unit is needed – it can be an old, sealed building or a steel covered container.

Blade the road: To level out an unpaved road by dragging a blade over the top.

Block heater: A device that allows you to plug your engine block into an electric source. There is nothing worse than a dead battery on a frigid prairie day.

Board Store: The Liquor Board store, where people can buy beer, wine and spirits.

The Bridge City: Saskatoon, a reference to the many bridges in the city that link the east and west sides over the South Saskatchewan River.

Buttcrack: Derogatory term for rural Saskatchewan. It's right next to the middle of nowhere.

Booty: A soaker. The unpleasant predicament one finds oneself in when water or muck is so deep that it overflows into your rubber boots.

Bumpering: Saskatchewan's own extreme sport! To go bumpering, grab the bumper of a moving vehicle and allow it pull you as it careens across the ice. This is dangerous and not at all recommended.

Bunny hug: A hooded fleece top that is either a pull over or has a front zipper. Elsewhere it's a hoodie.

Bush party: A large teen party, usually held clandestinely in a farm field and featuring a bonfire and under-aged drinking.

Chokecherry: A small nearly black berry that grows wild and as a cultivated fruit in Saskatchewan. The bitter fruit leaves a coating inside your mouth and is far tastier as a wine, jelly or syrup.

Take 5 HELEN MOURRE'S TOP FIVE WORDS TO DESCRIBE SASKATCHEWAN

Helen Mourre farms and writes from Sovereign, Saskatchewan. She has published two collections of short fiction; both were finalists in the Saskatchewan Book Awards. She has served on the boards of the Saskatchewan Writers Guild and The Sage Hill Writing Experience and has been a member of the University of Saskatchewan Senate. She is at work on her third book of short fiction, a group of stories about family relationships. Her writing focuses on the lives of rural people. She has taught fiction and poetry workshops throughout Saskatchewan.

1. **Land-locked**
2. **Wind-rocked**
3. **Light-shot**
4. **Awe-ful**
5. **Distance**

Coffee row: A morning coffee break. People from near and far gather at a local coffee shop for a cuppa and conversation. Topics of discussion invariably involve weather and/or politics.

Combine pilot: A bad driver with Saskatchewan license plates.

Cow or Buffalo chips: Dried, hardened pieces of cow or buffalo manure.

Dainties: Sweets of cookies usually prepared for a community or church luncheon.

Damp: In Saskatchewan this refers to grain with higher than 17 percent moisture content. Grain that is too damp will be tough.

Dugout: Most places know it as the shelter for a ball team, but in Saskatchewan it's also a farm's water supply.

Elevator: Most places it's the device that takes you from the lobby to the penthouse. In Saskatchewan it's a place for storing grain. Increasingly rare, efforts are made to preserve grain elevators.

Fall/fowl supper: A community supper held in the fall usually as a fund-raiser with donated fowl and all the fixings.

Farmer's tan: A distinctive tan pattern that covers just part of the body. Usually, it refers to the tan that farmers get whereby forearms are tanned while the upper arm, which was covered by a t-shirt, remains pale as a ghost.

Flatlander: Someone from the prairies.

Gibbled: Broken; dysfunctional.

Gitch: Men's underwear. For some reason, in Alberta they are referred to as gonch.

Great Western: A beer brewed in Saskatchewan.

Great White Combine: An intense and damaging hailstorm that wipes out a crop.

Grid Road: A dirt road that has a gravel top. It is so named because the roads were developed in a grid pattern.

Gopher: To be honest, the creatures that you see everywhere on the prairies are really Richardson's ground squirrels.

Gunny sac: A burlap sac used to transport or store vegetables or fruit. They are also used to cover plants when frosts come unseasonably late or early.

Gunny sac races: A popular children's game whereby children stand in a gunny sac, hold the top up to their waists and race to the finish line.

Hub City: Saskatoon.

Kaiser: A card game played with four people that includes tricks, bidding and trump. Only 32 of the 52 cards in a normal card deck are used.

L.B.: The Liquor Board or any Saskatchewan liquor store since they are all operated by the government with no private ownership.

Matrimonial cake: A square of dessert made with a flour and oatmeal crust and topping and filled with dates. Elsewhere, it's a date square.

M.F., The: Short for Maryfield, Saskatchewan, a little place in the south east part of the province.

Moose Javian: Someone who lives in Moose Jaw.

Miles: Canada went metric in 1970. Today, nearly four decades later, Saskatchewanians are on to the "new" system when it comes to the highways, but on rural roads directions are often still given in miles since the roads are on a grid that runs every mile by two miles.

P.A.: The short form of the city of Prince Albert.

Package pickup: An off-sale outlet that sells beer.

Peoples' Republic of Saskatchewan: A nickname for Saskatchewan, which pokes fun at its socialist tendencies.

Picking rocks: To clear a tilled field of rocks to protect farm machinery. For generations this grueling task was done by hand; today there is (thankfully) a machine to do it.

Pile o' Bones: Regina.

Prairie Oysters: This delicacy features the testicles of a bull. These tasty testes are usually fried.

Regina: The capital city of Saskatchewan. NOTE: It does not rhyme with Katrina.

Rubbing stone: A large stone used by animals to scratch themselves. In some parts of the country, they would have used a tree, but on the prairie where no trees were available, a stone did the trick.

Saskabush, Toontown: Yet more Saskatoon nicknames.

Saskatchewan chrome: Duct tape. It really can hold your bumper on.

Saskatchewan Day: A statutory holiday falling on the first Monday in August.

Saskatchewan Family Day: A statutory holiday first celebrated in February 2007. An NDP initiative, it was argued that the strong economy and the long period between New Year's Day and Easter warranted an extra day off with pay to celebrate family.

Saskatoon: Not the city, but an edible prairie berry that grows on low or high bushes. About the same size as a blueberry, in good years they can be found hanging like grapes. They can be enjoyed plain, with sugar and cream, in a pie or in a variety of other ways.

Shelterbelt: A row of trees planted around a farmhouse or on the edge of a field. The trees were free to farmers and were given out to encourage a decrease in soil erosion from wind and also maintain moisture by trapping blowing snow.

Slough: Refers to a naturally formed shallow freshwater pond.

Snowbirds: Canadians who winter down south, or the name of the Canadian military aerobatic flying team based in Moose Jaw.

Social: A party held prior to a wedding to celebrate the bride and groom.

Sodbuster/Drylander: The first European settlers to the prairie who built homes of sod or tilled the soil for the first time.

Soddie: An innovative home made from pieces of sod cut from the prairie and stacked on top of each other to make walls.

Speedy Creek: A nickname for the city of Swift Current.

Spits: Edible sunflower seeds, so named because when you shell the seed you must spit out the inedible shell.

Stubble jumper: A Saskatchewanian. This refers to the province's vast tracts of farmlands that, when harvested, leave stubble.

Supper: The evening meal. Dinner refers to lunch or the meal served at noon hour.

The centre of the universe: A derogatory term for Toronto.

The hood: North central Regina, a neighbourhood known for its high poverty, crime and unemployment rates, as well as its deplorable housing.

The Jaw: Nickname for the city of Moose Jaw.

The pen: This refers to the Federal Penitentiary in Prince Albert.

The Marble Palace: The nickname for the Saskatchewan legislature, located in Regina.

The roughies: The Saskatchewan Roughriders professional Canadian football team.

Vico: A small carton of chocolate milk.

Walleye: A fish also known as a pickerel.

Washboard: A gravel road that has many consecutive little bumps, not unlike an old fashioned washboard.

Winterpeg: The pet name for the only city that is colder than most of Saskatchewan most of the time.

The Natural World

Many associate Saskatchewan with images of flat, endless prairie and rolling fields of wheat. This terrain exists in the southern third of the province, but it does not tell the whole story. The central third of the province features boreal plains which boast mixed hardwood and coniferous forests. In the northern third, the boreal shield is covered with dense black spruce and moss – as well as poplar, jack pine and tamarack trees – and is dotted with lakes. In the north, there is a ribbon of the taiga shield, where the landscape is barren and supports only lichen woodlands and bogs.

The magnificence of these diverse ecosystems has long appealed to nature-lovers and conservationists alike. It also supports a wide array of amazing plants and animals.

GEOGRAPHIC ORIGINS

Except for the Cypress Hills area, Saskatchewan's landscape was shaped in the last million years as glacial erosion scoured the Precambrian shield in the northern part of the province, creating thousands of lakes, rivers and bogs. In the grasslands, fertile brown and black soils were deposited as the glaciers moved southwest across the land.

When ice sheets retreated they left behind moraines and glacial spillways, such as the Qu'Appelle Valley, which runs from west to east across southern Saskatchewan. Deposits in former pre-glacial lakes – bodies of water that formed in front of glaciers and later drained – create the expanses of flat land that dominate the prairie. The last glaciers melted in Saskatchewan's south about 16,000 to 18,000 years ago and in the north about 8,000 years ago.

THE RIVER

The North and South branches of the Saskatchewan River boast a length of 4,618 km. The northern branch originates in the Columbia Ice field of the Rockies, flows through Alberta and then into Saskatchewan. The South branch is born in southern Alberta at the junction of the Bow and Oldman Rivers. It flows northeast into Saskatchewan, past Saskatoon, running parallel to the North branch of the river until they converge approximately 50 km east of Prince Albert. The Saskatchewan then continues on into Manitoba where it empties into Lake Winnipeg.

The Saskatchewan River and its branches has long been the "highway" across western Canada, used first by Aboriginals and then by European fur traders. Not just a travel and communications route, the waters of the river system have provided much-needed crop irrigation on the drought-prone prairies. Today more than three million people live in the Saskatchewan River basin.

Sources: Encyclopedia of Saskatchewan (On-line); Canadian Encyclopedia; Canadian Council for Geographic Education.

They Said It

"Civilization says, 'Nature belongs to man.' The Indian says, 'No, man belongs to nature.'"
– Grey Owl, the English-born naturalist Archie Belaney.

LATITUDE AND LONGITUDE

Saskatchewan is a province in parallels. Three of Saskatchewan's borders fall directly on lines of latitude and longitude, while the fourth – the eastern boundary – follows a course of its own.

- Northern boundary: 60° north latitude.
- Southern boundary: 49°north latitude.
- Western boundary: 110° west longitude.
- Eastern boundary: Between 102° and 101°30' west longitude.

The capital city of Regina, in the province's southeast, is found at 50°27' north latitude, the same distance from the equator as Kiev, Ukraine.

Scotty the T. Rex

When school principal Robert Gebhardt and paleontologist Tim Tokaryk discovered a piece of vertebrae and then a chunk of jaw bone on an old cattle trail near Eastend in 1991, they knew they'd found something special. That evening, the pair celebrated with a bottle of scotch — giving "Scotty" the T-rex his name. Since then, nearly 70 percent of Scotty's skeleton has been uncovered, making him the most complete Tyrannosaurus Rex in Canada and one of only a dozen good skeletons in North America, the territory where T-rex roamed about 65 to 150 million years ago.

The Eastend T-rex Discovery Centre opened nearby in 2000, and it now hosts about 10,000 visitors each year. It has meant new prosperity for Eastend, a town with fewer than 600 people in an area of southwest Saskatchewan that is rich in paleontological sites. Bones from Scotty's tail, femur and hip, as well as a replica skull, are on display at the Discovery Centre. Scotty's . . . ah, er, poop . . . is also shockingly popular. A T-rex coprolite specimen (essentially fossilized dung) has spawned a gift shop t-shirt that reads "Coprolite Happens."

Take 5 SHARON BUTALA'S TOP FIVE SASKATCHEWAN NATURAL WONDERS

Born-and-bred in Saskatchewan, Sharon Butala is the prize winning author of more than fifteen books of both fiction and nonfiction. Although she was born in northern Saskatchewan, she has lived in small towns, Saskatoon, and has spent the last 30-plus years on the southern prairie.

Butala and her late husband, Peter Butala, donated an undisturbed tract of land to the Nature Conservancy of Canada to help create the Old Man on His Back Prairie and Heritage Conservation area. She says the idea of Saskatchewan as flat, solid cropland and boring couldn't be further from the truth.

1. **Cypress Hills**, at 1392 m, is the highest point between the Rocky Mountains and Labrador. While glaciers scoured the surrounding plain, they never reached this high and, as a result montane plant species found nowhere else on the prairies grow here. The view from Bald Butte across thousands of acres of prairie is stunning.

2. **Last Mountain Lake** in south central Saskatchewan is one thousands of lakes, in the province. It is home, however, to the first migratory bird sanctuary in North America (established in 1887). In the fall, thousands of sandhill cranes gather, many thousands more geese, and nearly as many ducks. Even non-bird-watchers are thrilled and awed, instantly converted, if not to bird watching, to appreciation of Saskatchewan's natural wonders.

3. **Athabasca Sand Dunes** in the far northwest of the province run for 100 km along the southern shore of Lake Athabasca, (the province's largest lake, and among the forty largest in the world), and reach up to 30 m in height. No other sand dunes in the world exist that far north. They are only accessible with guides, and on foot or by boat. (They are not the only dunes in the province: The Great Sand Hills are in southwestern Saskatchewan.)

4. Okay, so we do have grasslands. Located in west-central Saskatchewan is **Grasslands Park** (its southern limit the American border). Within its boundaries are badlands, high rolling hills, deep wooded coulees and a view of grass and sky so enormous that, standing on a high hill, you feel you're flying. Or you can visit the Old Man On His Back Prairie and Heritage Conservation Area west of the park, altitude, around 1,000 m. Watch the purebred plains buffalo herds at both places.

5. **Churchill** (Missinipe: The Great Water) River runs for more than 1600 km across the Canadian Shield in northern Saskatchewan, through immense, dense boreal forests, over and around rapids, creating 80 m high Nestowiak Falls, past lake after lake after lake. The fishing is superb, as is the animal-watching.

PHYSICAL SETTING
- Size: 651,036 km^2
- Land area: 591,670 km^2
- Water area: 59,366 km^2
- Saskatchewan covers 6.5 percent of Canada's total area
- Length: 1,225 km
- Width across the south: 630 km
- Width across the north: 445 km
- Highest elevation (Cypress Hills in the southwest): 1,392 m
- Lowest elevation (Lake Athabasca in the north): 213 m

Source: Encyclopedia of Saskatchewan (On-line); Canadian Encyclopedia.

PARKS
- Hectares of park land: 2 million +
- Number of provincial parks: 34
- Area of provincial parks: 1,148,287 ha^2
- Number of federal parks: 2

- Saskatchewan's provincial parks cover over 1,148,287 square hectares.
- Number of provincial parks: 34
- Historic sites: 8
- Recreation sites: 130
- Protected areas: 24

Cypress Hills Interprovincial Park: This, Canada's only park shared by two provinces – straddles the southern border between Saskatchewan and Alberta and features the highest elevation in the province. The park is home to four distinct habitats and a vast array of plant and animal life.

Douglas Provincial Park: 100 km northwest of Moose Jaw, it is home to sprawling active sand dunes and offers water sports on Lake Diefenbaker. The lake, created by the construction of the Gardiner and Qu'Appelle River dams on the South Saskatchewan River, stretches for 225 km and is part of three provincial parks.

Lac La Ronge: In the Canadian Shield north of Prince Albert sits Lac La Ronge Provincial Park, which boasts an international reputation as a wilderness canoeing paradise. The lake, Saskatchewan's fourth-largest, has more than 1,300 islands, and the province's oldest building, Holy Trinity Anglican Church, can only be reached by boat.

NATIONAL PARKS

Grasslands National Park celebrates the "badlands" prairie ecosystem. Grasslands is the first national park in Canada to preserve a portion of the mixed prairie grasslands. Eavesdrop on a prairie dog town or learn about how Sitting Bull took refuge here after the battle of the Little Bighorn in 1876.

Bio GREY OWL

From his cabin in Prince Albert National Park, Grey Owl, Canada's best-known conservationist, enthralled the world with his eloquent call for wilderness preservation. After his death, he was exposed as an Englishman posing as an Apache.

Grey Owl was Archie Belaney. He was born in England in 1888. At 17, he moved to northern Ontario where he learned to canoe and trapped and guided for a living. There he adopted the persona of Grey Owl, claiming to be the son of a Scottish father and Apache mother.

Twenty years later, an incident changed his life. After killing a mother beaver in a trap, he discovered her two babies which he adopted and named Jelly Roll and Rawhide. Urged by his wife, Anahareo, he stopped trapping and picked up a pen. Under the name Grey Owl, he wrote passionate articles about conservation. He caught the attention of the Dominion Parks Service and was employed as a naturalist in Saskatchewan's Prince Albert National Park.

In 1931, Grey Owl, Anahareo and their pet beavers moved to a cabin in the park. There, they were visited by hundreds of tourists each summer. He traveled Canada and his native England, preaching a conservation message. His travels and hard work took a toll on his health, and he died of pneumonia in 1938. Shortly after his death, a newspaper in North Bay, ON, revealed his true identity.

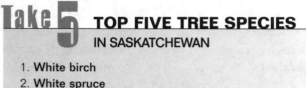

Take 5 **TOP FIVE TREE SPECIES**
IN SASKATCHEWAN

1. White birch
2. White spruce
3. Black spruce
4. Jack pine
5. Trembling aspen

Prince Alberta National Park protects a slice of the boreal forest. It is home to a free-ranging herd of plains bison, the only fully protected nesting colony of white pelicans in Canada, and contains the lakeside cabin of conservationist Grey Owl.

WOODLAND

More than half of Saskatchewan is forested – trees cover approximately 355,000 km². The dominant softwood species include balsam fir, black spruce, jack pine and white spruce while hardwood forests feature balsam poplar, trembling aspen and white birch.

MOTHER NATURE'S PRUNING

Each year for the last decade, Saskatchewan saw an average 644 forest fires burn about 414,000 hectares. Just over 50 percent of the fires in that period were started by lightning strikes, while the rest were caused by human activities. In 2006, there were fewer fires than average – just

They Said It

> "Silence and solitude – the finest gifts Saskatchewan has to offer bedevilled modern man."
>
> – **Edward McCourt, 1968**

501 – but those fires burned more than 1.2 million hectares. Back in 1998, 1,266 blazes burned about 960,000 hectares. That year the province spent $107 million to fight the many fires.

Source: Saskatchewan Environment.

The Great Gopher Derby of 2002-03

Shooting gophers is something of a right of passage in rural Saskatchewan as valuable prairie fields are often overrun with these unpopular rodents, officially known as the Richardson ground squirrel.

In 2002, the Saskatchewan Wildlife Federation (SWF) took action when a particularly large gopher population was plaguing farmers. A province-wide gopher derby was launched to the delight of farmers and the outrage of animal rights activists. Gopher-culling enthusiasts from all over the province went on a gopher hunting mission. Local chapters of the SWF were flooded with gopher tails by the thousands. The number of complaints from protesters were not far behind.

The derby even brought in a small group of tourists from Wichita, Kansas, who paid $1,200 US each to be outfitted for the event. The following year, these tourist-hunters returned in even greater numbers. Meanwhile, activists continued to cry cruelty at the more than 61,000 rodents killed in the inaugural derby that saw the winning hunter alone offer up about 3,000 tails, all taken from one farm.

In 2004, critics claimed victory when the hunt was not renewed. SWF officials insist that its cancellation had little to do with the backlash – wet conditions that year drastically reduced the gopher population, negating the need for a hunt.

While the official hunt is over, local gopher-hunting contests across Saskatchewan continue to keep the pesky population in check and local animal welfare activists continue to complain. As for the gophers, it's safe to say that, derby or no derby, the critters will forever be popping their little heads from their prairie holes.

Sources: Saskatchewan Wildlife Federation; Saskatoon Star Phoenix.

Take 5   HAYLEY WICKENHEISER'S TOP FIVE FAVOURITE THINGS ABOUT GROWING UP PLAYING HOCKEY IN SASKATCHEWAN

A native of Shaunavon, Saskatchewan, Hayley Wickenheiser began her hockey career on the Canadian Women's National Team at just 15 years old. She has since led the team to two Olympic gold medals, an Olympic silver medal and five Women's World Hockey Championship titles. Wickenheiser was also the first woman to ever notch a point in a men's professional game. She continues to excel in her sport today and plans to play in the 2010 Olympics.

1. **Rink Burgers and Fries:** I loved my ritual of no junk food at the rink, but a cheeseburger and fries was allowed every Saturday. Rinks like Shaunavon, Hodgeville, Eastend, etc, have some of the best food you'll find.

2. **Ice time:** Ice time was always available at the local rink to get out there. Two-hour practices hardly exist today, but they did when I was a kid.

3. **Develops Character:** Many of the rinks I played in were colder inside than out. I can remember playing in Consul and wearing toques and mitts under my equipment to stay warm. We played in any and every condition and it toughened us up! I was also often the only girl and changed in places like boiler rooms, closets and bathrooms.

4. **Only show in town:** I can remember being a kid in a final of some minor hockey tournament and the rink was filled to capacity. The whole town supports its teams and it's a sense of belonging for the community.

5. **Outdoor Rink:** My dad built one in our backyard for all the neighborhood kids and even flooded a path from the back door to the rink in Shaunavon, so you could skate from the house where it was warm. The outdoor rink is a bit of a lost art, but it is the place where I developed a love and passion for the game and there is no other place I love to be than a beautiful starry night on the outdoor rink.

Take 5 — TOP FIVE GRASSES
NATIVE TO SASKATCHEWAN

1. **Northern wheat grass**
2. **Blue grama**
3. **June grass**
4. **Needle-and-thread**
5. **Western porcupine grass**

CROOKED TREES

The clump of aspen trees on Skip and Linda Magowan's farm, near Hafford, is like something out of a foreboding Tim Burton film. The aspens – located northwest of Saskatoon — grow twisted and gnarled unlike any other aspen trees in the area. Indeed, they are unlike any stand of aspens anywhere. That's according to Rick Sawatsky, a Plant Sciences technician at the University of Saskatchewan and the only person to successfully propagate a crooked tree away from the original grove.

Because they can be propagated elsewhere, something in the plant — not something in the soil – must be responsible for the trees' crooked growth pattern, a pattern called "weeping." There is no proof that the trait is genetic, but it's a safe bet. It is speculated that the characteristic may be the result of a gene that is carried but only very rarely expressed. This is an especially intriguing idea because this proposed "weeping" gene puts the trees at a disadvantage to trees that stand straight.

Extensive local lore surrounds the subject of what might have cause a genetic mutation in the trees. Perhaps it was some supernatural force, or radiation from an alien spaceship.

They Said It

"Remember you belong to Nature, not it to you."

– Grey Owl

Take 5 — SASKATCHEWAN'S FIVE LARGEST LAKES (AREA)

1. **Lake Athabasca** (7,935 km^2)
2. **Reindeer Lake** (6,650 km^2)
3. **Wollaston Lake** (2,681 km^2)
4. **Cree Lake** (1,434 km^2)
5. **Lac La Ronge** (1,413 km^2)

FARM COUNTRY

Saskatchewan has 44,329 farms covering 64.3 million acres – about a third of the province. The average farm size was 1,449 acres. Of the 64.3 million acres, 57.5 percent grew crops, 19.9 percent was natural pasture, 9.3 percent was summer fallow and 7.5 percent was tamed or seeded pasture land.

In comparison the province has 43 percent of Canada's cultivated land, 42 percent of Canada's cropped land, 69 percent of Canada's summer fallow land, 34 percent of the nation's seeded pasture land and 34 percent of Canada's natural pasture land.

Source: Government of Saskatchewan.

RULES OF OWNERSHIP

Until 2002, Canadian residents could own up to 320 acres of Saskatchewan farmland. Now there are no limits on the amount that Canadian residents (who reside in Canada 183 or more days a year) can own. Non-residents, however, are restricted to just 10 acres, but can receive approval to own more through the Farm Land Security Board.

Source: Prairie Centre Policy Institute

Did you know...

that Saskatchewan has more freshwater, by area, than Alberta and British Columbia combined?

Take 5 TOP FIVE LONGEST SASKATCHEWAN RIVERS (LENGTH)

1. **Saskatchewan River** (1,939 km, to head of Bow River)
2. **Churchill River** (1,609 km)
3. **South Saskatchewan River** (1,392 km to head of Bow River)
4. **North Saskatchewan River** (1,287 km)
5. **Qu'Appelle River** (430 km)

GRASSHOPPERS

These crop-ravaging prairie pests, known locally as "hoppers," are well-suited to Saskatchewan, where dry weather conditions in the spring and early summer provide ideal living conditions for the insects. Grasshoppers are among the province's most prevalent crop pests, primarily in the grassland region. Of the 70 species of grasshoppers found in Saskatchewan, however, only four pose a real problem.

The province can expect a major outbreak of grasshoppers every 10 to 12 years, causing tens of millions of dollars in crop damage, especially to cereal grains. Local infestations of the insects can last several years.

WATER, WATER EVERYWHERE

About 12% of Saskatchewan is covered by water. In all, the province has 328,345 lakes larger than one hectare.

Source: Saskatchewan Watershed Authority

Did you know...

that Wollaston Lake, in the province's northeast, is the largest lake in the world to drain naturally in two directions? The lake drains north to the Mackenzie River basin and east to Hudson Bay.

Take 5 — TOP FIVE ENDANGERED BIRDS AND MAMMALS

1. Burrowing Owl
2. Piping Plover
3. Sage Grouse
4. Whooping Crane
5. Swift Fox

GOOD FOR WHAT AILS YA

Saskatchewan is home to two natural spas, one at Moose Jaw, the other at Watrous. Their waters, alleged to have healing properties, have attracted bathers for decades.

The waters of both spas reach a delightful 45°C and are filled with curative, healthful minerals – something the First People recognized for centuries. The water is rich in epsom salts, glauber's salts, sodium, potassium, calcium, magnesium chloride, bicarbonate, sulphate, boron, bromine, fluoride, silicon, and strontium as trace elements. In addition, Manitou Springs contains iron, aluminum, silica and sulfur – this gives it its distinctive colour.

Did you know...

that the oldest waterfowl refuge in North America is Saskatchewan's Last Mountain Lake Bird Sanctuary? Reserved by the federal government in 1887, the refuge now includes more than 15,600 hectares. Over 280 bird species visit the sanctuary during migration.

Take 5 — TOP FIVE ENDANGERED OR THREATENED PLANTS

1. Hairy Prairie Clover
2. Sand Verbena
3. Tiny Cryptanthe
4. Western Spiderwort
5. Slender Mouse-ear-cress

PRAIRIE POTHOLES

Low-lying, water-collecting pools dot southwest Saskatchewan's grasslands. Although their water levels vary, sloughs, marshes and potholes can sustain a host of plant and animals. They also serve the practical purpose of providing clean water for irrigation and for the livestock that graze in grassland pastures.

AN ODD PRAIRIE BEACON

Saskatchewan is one of two Canadian provinces (the other is Alberta) without any coastline. It may, therefore, seem strange that Saskatchewan is home to a real live lighthouse. Built as a tourist attraction in Cochin, the lighthouse was erected on the top of Pirot Hill overlooking Jackfish Lake. At 11.5 m tall, visitors have to climb 153 steps to enjoy the vistas.

THE NIGHT THE SKY RAINED DUCKS

Between 9:30 pm and 2 am, on November 7-8, 1940, residents of Foam Lake were dumbfounded as hundreds of plump Bafflehead ducks crash landed in the community. Residents scrambled with their gunny sacks to collect the free gifts of food.

The birds were en route to their Atlantic coast wintering grounds when they crashed to earth. No one knows for sure why they plummeted to their deaths, but it has been proposed that the freezing rain reported in the region that night may have contributed. When ice-coated streets were illuminated by street lights, it is possible that the errant fowl mistook the roads for icy rivers and made their deadly mistake.

AKA THE GOPHER
The animal known to most Saskatchewan residents as the gopher is actually the Richardson's ground squirrel, millions of which are found in Saskatchewan. An enemy of early homesteaders and modern-day farmers and ranchers, ground squirrels feed on forage grasses and legumes, crops and native grasses. They prefer grasslands with sparse vegetation – an environment which allows them to see predators – and fare particularly well when making their tunnel homes in city parks, over-grazed pastures and at the edges of cultivated fields.

ATHABASCA SAND DUNES
At heights of 30 m and lengths of 400 m to 1,500 m, the Athabasca Sand Dunes is the largest active dune field in North America and is the most northerly active dune in the world. Found in northwest Saskatchewan near the 60th parallel, they extend east from the Alberta border in a 100 km strip along the shores of Lake Athabasca.

The sand dunes are about 8,000 years old, formed during the last glacial period when glaciers turned sandstone to powder. The dune field began as a delta in a giant freshwater lake but over centuries the wind has formed the sand into overwhelming and expansive formations.

Large parts of the dunes are still unstable, moving with the prevailing winds and slowly smothering the adjacent forest. In other locations, the dunes gradually reveal long-buried forest.

The dunes are also an evolutionary puzzle, home to about 50 rare plants species as well as 10 plant species or varieties found nowhere else in the world. The area was designated a crown reserve in the 1970s and became a provincial park in 1992. The wilderness park now covers almost 2,000 km^2, and Parks Canada calls it one of the most important natural regions of the country.

It is a delicate environment and visitors must follow strict guidelines. No plants, trees or artifacts can be collected. The park is isolated – it has no communities, permanent residents, services, facilities or roads of any kind, and visitors must access the dunes by float plane.

Sources: Encyclopedia of Saskatchewan (On-line); Saskatchewan Environment; Canadian Parks and Wilderness Society.

Weblinks

Nature Saskatchewan

www.naturesask.ca/

This non-profit charitable organization promotes appreciation and understanding of Saskatchewan's natural world. The website includes nature photography and information about stewardship and education programs.

Saskatchewan Environmental Society

www.environmentalsociety.ca/

The website includes resources and information about the Society, a non-profit group committed to supporting and encouraging sustainability through energy conservation and protection of natural resources.

Saskatchewan Environment

www.se.gov.sk.ca/

The website of this provincial government department provides access to information on hunting and fishing, forestry, parks and more.

Canadian Parks and Wilderness Society (CPAWS)

www.cpaws-sask.org/

The website for the Saskatchewan chapter of CPAWS, an organization committed to nature preservation, includes up-to-date information on boreal forest and grasslands conservation as well as ways to get involved in environmental campaigns.

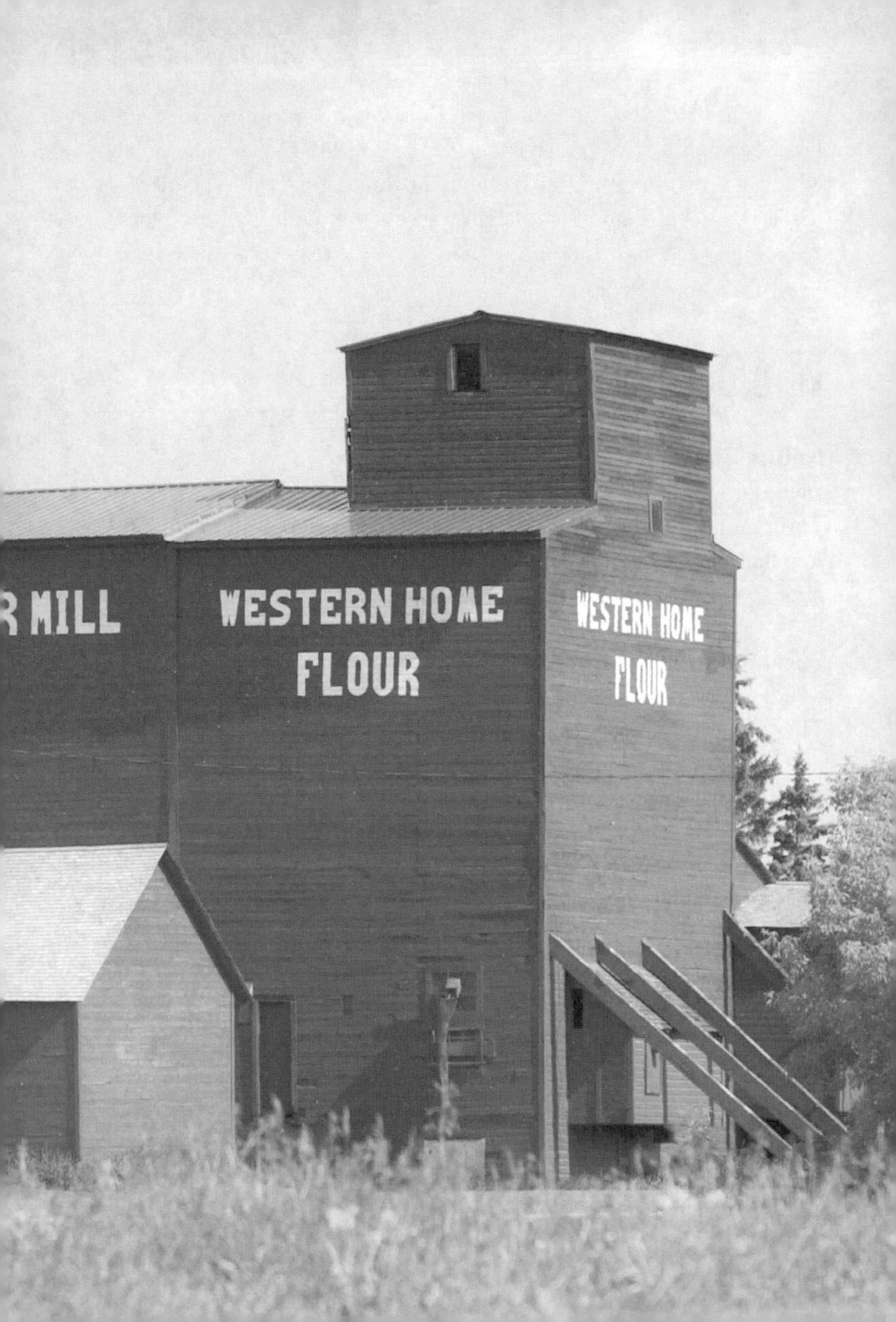
R MILL
WESTERN HOME
FLOUR
WESTERN HOME
FLOUR

Place Names

The map of Saskatchewan offers ready evidence of the many people who have called it home over the past 10,000 years. Names reflect the enduring presence of the First People and offer a lasting testament to the geography and natural beauty of the place. Other more recent names record the histories of newcomers who attached to their new home memories of a far-off homeland. Still others commemorate individuals famous, or not so famous, whose lives have been immortalized in dots on a map.

Interestingly, many places got their names in a far more arbitrary way. These were chosen by Grand Trunk Pacific railway workers. Locations placed seven miles apart – about the distance that a team of horses could travel a day – were named by workers following an alphabetical scheme that started in Manitoba with Alpha.

Amazon: This former Canadian Pacific Railway siding southeast of Saskatoon was named for a Royal Navy F Class destroyer, which was launched in 1908.

Avonlea: This village south of Regina was named for Anne's fictional home town in Lucy Maud Montgomery's book, *Anne of Green Gables.* The book was wildly popular around the time of the village's naming in 1911.

Balgonie: Located just east of Regina, the town of Balgonie is named for the 14th century Balgonie castle in Fife, Scotland.

Battleford: This town, the former capital of the Northwest Territories, rests on the south side of the North Saskatchewan River near where it joins the Battle River. It is so named because the Cree and Blackfoot, long-term enemies, often sparred on the river, which they called "fighting water."

Buffalo Narrows: On the narrows between Churchill Lake and Little Peter Pond Lake (Little Buffalo Lake), the town is known as a spot where First People used to drive bison to the narrows where they could be readily killed.

Carrot River: Located in northeast Saskatchewan, the town is so named because the first homesteaders to settler here (in 1911) found wild carrots growing along the river. Carrot River became a village in 1941 and was incorporated as a town in 1948.

Climax: This village was named after Climax, Minnesota, the home of a homesteader who, like many other Americans, settled in southern Saskatchewan in the early 20th century. The Minnesota Climax is named after a chewing tobacco brand.

Congress: This hamlet, located southwest of Moose Jaw, has a CPR List name likely honouring the U.S. legislature. Streets in this very Canadian community rather oddly include presidential names like Washington, Wilson, Taft, and Roosevelt.

Crocus: Although you won't find it on a map, there is no better-known Saskatchewan town. Crocus is the fictional town immortalized by author W.O. Mitchell in his wildly popular radio series, "Jake and the Kid."

Take 5 SHEILA COLES' TOP FIVE REASONS TO MOVE TO, AND SETTLE IN, SASKATCHEWAN

The voice of Sheila Coles is recognized throughout Saskatchewan. She hosts the CBC Radio Saskatchewan Morning Edition heard weekdays beginning at 6:00 a.m. Coles moved to the province some twenty years ago having made stops in Winnipeg, Vancouver, Edmonton, St. Johns, Beijing, Barbados and Jersey (Channel Islands.) After all those, the journalist, who was born in England, chose to stay in Regina where she lives with her husband and three children.

1. **Regina's Cathedral Area (where I live):** It's a village within a city, with a vibrant arts scene, lovely bistros and coffee shops, and funky boutiques. It's full of affordable, beautiful old homes a quarter of the cost of similar housing in downtown Vancouver.

2. **Regina's Wascana Park:** One of North America's largest urban parks, complete with a lake right in the middle of town. It's a lovely, peaceful place to run, walk, cycle or simply be alone with your thoughts. I head for the park at least a couple of times a week, year-round.

3. **Accessible Arts:** Professional, high calibre theatre-in-the-round and a first-rate symphony orchestra. The bonus is many symphony musicians are available to teach music to Regina kids and the legacy continues in the form of the fabulous South Saskatchewan Youth Orchestra! In Saskatoon. From the orchestra, to Persephone Theatre, to Shakespeare on the Saskatchewan, the arts scene thrives as well.

4. **Northern Lakes:** Shhhhh, don't tell anyone, because many of our lakes and forest are still pristine and largely undiscovered. A canoe trip on the Churchill River system is the best therapy in the world. Living outside, checking out the wildlife, feasting on wild blueberries — it's all medication for the soul.

5. **Outstanding Skies:** Our license plates say it: Land of Living Skies. From spectacular sunsets and sunrises, to dramatic prairie storms, to the magical northern lights. Who needs T.V. when the sky provides a new show every day? From most vantage points, you can still see the stars.

They Said It

Cut Knife: This town west of Battleford is named for the Sarcee chief, "Kiskihkoman," meaning cut, or broken, knife, who was defeated by the Cree in a 19th century hilltop battle in what is now the nearby Poundmaker Reserve. Cut Knife is home to the world's largest Tomahawk, a symbol of friendship between the Aboriginal and non-Aboriginal populations who call the town home.

Davidson: This town, located midway between Saskatoon and Regina, is named for Colonel Andrew Duncan Davidson of Minneapolis, the president of the Saskatchewan Valley Land Company. Between 1902 and his death in 1920, Davidson's company settled 50,000 families, most of them American, along the route between Saskatchewan's two largest cities.

Elbow: This village, located between Saskatoon and Regina on Diefenbaker Lake, gets its name from the abrupt curve in the South Saskatchewan River where it veers about 300 degrees, resembling a bent arm.

They Said It

Estevan: This southeastern city got its name from the first president of the Canadian Pacific Railway, George Stephen. Estevan, a variant of Stephen's surname, was registered as his telegraph address.

The Queen City

The site of Saskatchewan's capital city was once a Cree and Métis hunting area. Native hunters, believing that the important mammal would not leave as long as its bones were there, collected bison bones at the site in order to ensure hunting success. Aptly, the locale was first called "Pile o' Bones."

In 1882, "Pile o' Bones" made headlines when it was selected by Edgar Dewdney, the lieutenant-governor of the North-West Territories, as the territory's headquarters. A waterless, treeless and flat location, boasting only a small spring run-off creek, Dewdney's choice caused a national scandal. Without much to recommend it as a settlement site, the locale was too coincidentally near to land Dewdney had purchased for himself which was adjacent to the planned route of the CPR. Many believed that Battleford, the previous territorial capital, which had been located on rolling parklands with an ample water supply, was a more prudent location.

Dewdney's choice stuck, however, and from this somewhat shaky beginning grew the present-day city of Regina. The village was named in 1882 after Queen Victoria, whose full name was Victoria Regina and two years later was designated a town. In 1885, the new town earned national headlines when it was home to the famous trial and controversial execution of Métis leader, Louis Riel, for his part in the 1885 uprising. On June 19, 1903 the community of 3,000 was proclaimed a city and on May 23, 1906, Regina became the provincial capital.

Today, Regina is the hub of provincial government and the major commercial centre of southern Saskatchewan. Not just a financial centre of banks and skyscrapers, Regina is also an oasis of greenery and is home to more than 100 parks. This is particularly remarkable given that all trees, shrubs and other plants are not native to the prairie region. They have been planted and nurtured by hand – all 300,000 of them.

Fort Qu'Appelle: A Cree word "kab-tep-was" meaning "the river that calls." A legend tells of a Cree man who was paddling his canoe on the way to his wedding. He heard his name called out. It was the voice of his bride who was still many days travel away. He answered, "Who calls?" A spirit echoed, "Who calls?" He then hurried home only to find out that his bride had died. The last words she spoke were his name. The French settlers who came to Saskatchewan named the river Qu'Appelle, meaning "qui appelle" or, "who calls?" The town along the banks of the Qu'Appelle in south eastern Saskatchewan shares this name.

Good Spirit Lake: This provincial park north of Yorkton was known to Europeans for about 150 years as Devil or Devil's Lake. The Cree name for the lake, "manitow," means "good spirit," but to some Europeans, such a spirit, clearly not of the Christian variety, was considered the work of the devil. Over time, the name Good Spirit Lake took over, although the Devil's Lake post office was open until 1954.

Ibsen Lake: This lake near Weyburn was given a CPR list name honouring famed Norwegian playwright, Henrik Ibsen.

Indian Head: The beauty of this town east of Regina belies a name that stems from a rather ghastly set of circumstances. Indian Head Hill was a name assigned to it by the Cree to commemorate the horrific small pox epidemic of 1837-38. Many Cree perished of the disease and their skeletons – including skulls – littered the area.

Jamieson Lake: This lake in northeastern Saskatchewan lake is named for Mel Jamieson, the first non-native resident at nearby Wollaston Lake. Jamieson was a well-known fisher, trapper and taxidermist.

Paris of the Prairies

Saskatchewan's largest city rests beside the South Saskatchewan River in the heart of the prairies. It gets its name from a Cree word, "mis-sask-guah-too-min," which refers to the tasty wild berry found along its riverbanks. The area now known as Saskatoon has been inhabited for some 8,000 years by the Plains Cree. The first European settlers arrived in 1883, when a group of Toronto Methodists saw in Prime Minister John A. Macdonald's offer of free land a golden opportunity to escape the evils of the urban liquor traffic. In 1881, 3,100 would-be colonists signed up for more than two million acres. Within two years, Methodist minister-turned-entrepreneur John Lake arrived with his group of new settlers.

The South Saskatchewan River that bisects the city first attracted the settlers and it remains Saskatoon's pride and joy. Seven bridges span the South Saskatchewan, earning for the city the nickname "Paris of the Prairies." Its 300 acres of riverbank parklands provide a network of trails for walking, biking and jogging. You can even watch white pelicans fish in the fast flow at the base of the river's weir and each year Saskatoonians compete in a contest to predict the date on which these elegant birds will return to the city.

Today, Saskatoon boasts of its big city convenience and small town spirit. A "university town," it is regarded as a safe, clean and friendly city where the arts figure prominently. Saskatoon is home to a number of festivals, a symphony orchestra, and three professional theatre companies.

Saskatoon's economy is centred on agricultural services, education, mining administration and a flourishing high tech industry. In fact, it is one of the top ten cities in the world for agricultural biotechnology and local companies often win in competition against firms from around the world. In recent years, Saskatoon has become a city of world renowned science as it is home to the Canadian Light Source. This national source for synchrotron light research is one of only six third-generation synchrotrons in the world. When it is fully operational in 2008, Canadian Light Source will attract 2,000 researchers from around the world each year. At a cost of $175 million this largest single science project ever undertaken in Canada has put Saskatoon on Canada's high tech map.

Kahkewistahaw: This First Nation locale west of Regina is named for Chief Kahkewistahaw, or "one that flies around." Kahkewistahaw was one of the original signatories of Treaty 4 in 1874. He wanted reserve land in the game-rich Cypress Hills, but the federal government instead forced the band to accept land intended for agriculture in the Qu'Appelle valley.

Kandahar: This hamlet east of Saskatoon was named by the CPR for Frederick Sleigh Roberts, a British general who won a rare victory on Afghan soil in 1879 after a march from Kabul to Kandahar to relieve British forces. He was knighted in 1882 as Baron Roberts of Kandahar.

La Ronge: The origin of the name of the largest community in northern Saskatchewan is unclear, but it is usually believed to come from the French verb ronger, meaning to gnaw, likely a reference to the plentiful beavers in the area.

Last Mountain Lake: Cree legend holds that before the world was complete, the Great Spirit scooped out a long lake and used the earth to make one last mountain. Last Mountain Lake, located north of Regina, is home to a First Nation reserve and a bird sanctuary that offers protection to nine of Canada's threatened bird species. The lake is also known as Long Lake, or Kinookimaw, which is the name of the resort near the southern end of the lake.

Lloydminster: Straddling the Alberta-Saskatchewan border, this city is named for Rev. George Exton Lloyd. Originally known as Britannia Settlement, the community was first settled in 1903 by 3,000 British settlers led by Rev. Isaac Barr. On arriving in their new land, the settlers were angry as they felt they had been mislead by Barr about prairie conditions. Outraged, they deposed their leader and named Lloyd, their chaplain, in his stead. The people unanimously agreed to change the name of their community in honour of their new leader to Lloydminster, meaning Lloyd's church. The community was split down the middle in 1905 when the provinces of Alberta and Saskatchewan were created.

Love: Sadly for all you romantics, this place name origin is not as touching as it seems. This village northeast of Prince Albert shares the surname of the chief of Canadian Pacific's passenger bureau in Winnipeg.

Moose Jaw: Several explanations — all connected to Aboriginal names for the place — describe the origin of this town name. One version suggests that the First Nation word Moosoochapiskanissippi means "the river shaped like the jaw of a moose," and so the town may have been named from the creek that flowed through the settlement. Another version of its origin says that the name comes from the Native word, Moosoochapiskun, meaning "the place where the white man mended the cart with the jawbone of the moose." Yet a third theory is that the name came from the Cree word moosegaw which means "warm breezes." In the winter Moose Jaw is warmer that the surrounding communities.

Mozart: When the CPR was built in this small farming community, a settler proposed that the town be named in honour of her favorite composer. Incidentally, streets in the small town have also been named for composers.

Naicam: The name of this town, which is located 200 km north of Regina, is pretty straightforward and stems from a combination of the names of two Canadian Pacific Railway contractors. The last names of the two men, Naismith and Camerson, were merged to form "Naicam." Not long after the CPR arrived in 1921, Naicam was incorporated as a village.

Nokomis: This town's name refers to Hiawatha's grandmother in Henry Wadsworth Longfellow's epic 1855 poem, "The Song of Hiawatha." Florence Mary Halstead selected the name in 1906 for a post office she established in her sod home near the eventual townsite in south central Saskatchewan. The word nookomis means "grandmother" in the Ojibwe language.

Old Wives Lake: This lake, located 30 km southwest of Moose Jaw, earns its name from Cree legend. According to the story, when a lakeside Cree encampment feared a Blackfoot attack, women elders offered to keep the fires burning and drum throughout the night, allowing the rest of their people to escape into the darkness. When the Blackfoot attacked the next morning they found only the old women whom they killed. It is said that on windy nights you can still hear the old women's cries.

Orkney: George Spence, a prominent early settler of this southwestern hamlet, named his Saskatchewan town in the southwest corner of the province for the land of his birth — the Orkney Islands near Scotland's northern coast.

Prince Albert: This city at the centre of the province was once a First Nations meeting place known as kistahpinanihk. In 1776, fur trader Peter Pond built a fort, just west of the present-day city. Almost a century later, in 1866, a group of Presbyterian colonists joined the local Métis and First Nation population. The colonists' leader, Rev. James Nisbet, gave the town its current handle to honour the husband and consort of Queen Victoria.

Quill Lake: This village east of Saskatoon was named because the shores of the nearby Quill Lakes, home to a migratory bird breeding ground, are often littered with the seasonal visitors' feathers and quills.

Saltcoats: Located in southeastern Saskatchewan, Saltcoats was first called Stirling. In 1882 it got its new handle, named after the home base of the Allen Steamship Line, the company that brought many of the community's first residents from Scotland.

Shamrock: Although most of the original settlers of this southwestern village were from Iceland, this name likely honours the several Irish families who settled in the district.

Swift Current: This southwest city takes its name from the Swift Current Creek, which flows through it and empties into the Saskatchewan River. The Cree knew the river as "kisiskâciwan" — the same word they used for the Saskatchewan River — which means "it flows swiftly." In the early 19th century French fur traders called the creek "Riviere Au Courant," meaning swift current. In 1881, a community named Swift Current was officially established with the arrival of the CPR. The first settlers arrived a year later and in 1903 the community gained village status and four years later became a town.

Tangleflags: Located northeast of Lloyminster, the name of this rural community was coined in recognition of its first settlers' array of nationalities. It is home to the Tangleflags oil field.

Unity: This town southwest of the Battlefords is believed to be named after Unity, Wisconsin, perhaps the place of origin of some of its settlers. The town, however, sits on Grand Trunk Pacific's 1907-08 main Alphabet line and so it is possible that the name was one of convenience — "unity" may simply be a chosen "U" word.

Val Marie: This southwestern Saskatchewan village was originally a Métis settlement. In 1910, missionary priest Father Claude Passaplan brought settlers here from France. The name, meaning "Valley of Mary," honours the Virgin Mary.

Valparaiso: Originally the village was to be called Beaver Flats. Since the place name Beaver was very popular at the time, the search for a unique name began. Valparaiso means "Paradise Valley" in Spanish, and was named after Valparaiso, Chile.

Vanguard: This village in the province's southwest was named in 1912 because its location was, for several decades until the 1930s, the head, or "vanguard" of the CPR line. The town is well known for the nearby Vanguard Hutterite Colony.

Victory: This rural municipality based in Beechy, northeast of Swift Current, was named in 1919 to celebrate the Allied victory in the First World War.

Wanuskewin: The Cree word wanaskewin means "seeking peace of mind." This site, just north of Saskatoon, has been a gathering place for First Nations people for 6,000 or more years. Since 1992 it has been home to a National Historic Site that explores the history and culture of the First People who have called this place home.

Warman: This bedroom community north of Saskatoon is named for American journalist Cyrus Warman, who chronicled the day-to-day story of the construction of the Canadian Northern railway in 1905 and 1906. When Warman was asked to name two stations on the railway, he chose Dana and Vonda after two of his children.

Warmley: The name of this community in southeastern Saskatchewan has nothing to do with ambient temperature. Originally, it was called Yankeetown in tribute to the origin of A. S. Porter, who surveyed a town site and attempted to create his own estate. Within a month the community was renamed Warmley in honour of Porter's wife, who had been raised in Warmley Park in England.

Weyburn: Several theories explain how this city, located southeast of Regina and incorporated in 1913, got its name. It may be named after the brother-in-law of a railroad contractor, or the name may come from Old English, a combination of "weoh" and "burna" which, together, means shrine by a creek. Still another story asserts that an exploring Scot exclaimed, "Wee burn," meaning small river, as he came across the Souris River. Weyburn was the birthplace of famed Canadian author W. O. Mitchell.

Whitecap: Dakota First Nation Chief Wapahaska (or White Cap) and his band came from the Minnesota area and settled south of Saskatoon. Wapahaska was unwillingly caught up in Louis Riel's 1885 resistance, but was later acquitted of treason. Although Wapahaskas' group didn't sign a treaty, the band received reserve land along the South Saskatchewan River. The community was known as Moose Woods until 1995.

Xerxes: No one is sure how this rather oddly named community got its name. Many believe, however, that the Xerxes railroad siding was located northwest of Unity to complete the Alphabet line of the Grand Trunk's Pacific line.

Yorkton: This city, located northeast of Regina, is named after the York County, Ontario settlement group that founded York City in 1882. It was renamed Yorkton to prevent confusion with the Ontario community.

Zealandia: This town southwest of Saskatoon was originally to be named Brock, but residents preferred to use New Zealand in honour of an early settler from that country, Thomas Englebrecht. Eventually they decided on Zealandia.

Source: Geographic Names of Saskatchewan

Weather and Climate

In "Big Sky Country," where agriculture is king, weather is a going concern. You can expect sunny skies – Saskatchewan gets more sunshine than any other province. But you can also expect wild weather – summer storms, winter blizzards and extreme temperatures are no strangers.

Saskatchewan summers are warm and dry with high temperatures in the mid-30s°C. Autumn brings average temperatures in the 8°C range in September, dipping to a chilly -11°C by November. Winters are cold with slight amounts of snow. January temperatures hover around the -30°C mark in the north, but the occasional Chinook blows in from the west, tempering the sting of such frigid air. Spring is pleasant, but noted for its brevity.

AT A GLANCE
- Warmest Month: July
- Coldest month: January
- Wettest Month: June and July compete for this claim, depending on where you are in the province.

They Said It

PRECIPITATION

- Annual precipitation rain and snow: 427.81 mm
- Annual rainfall: 311.14 mm
- Annual snowfall: 144.98 cm
- Percentage of precipitation that falls as snow: 34

Source: Environment Canada.

AND THE WINNER IS . . .

Highest temperature: 45°C at Yellow Grass and Midale on July 5, 1937. This the hottest day ever recorded in Canada.

Lowest temperature: -56.7°C, at Prince Albert on February 1, 1893.

Windiest day: On October 4, 1976 at Melfort, when maximum hourly wind speeds reached 142 km/hr.

Wettest day: On August 3, 1985, 380 mm of rain fell on Parkman.

Snowiest days: The two snowiest days in the province happened in March. On March 15, 1941 at Semans and again on March 24, 1979 at Lac la Ronge, 61 cm fell.

Source: Environment Canada.

Did you know...

that during the winter of 1955-56, the temperature in southern Saskatchewan remained below -10°C for a record 129 days?

SPLEENY FORECAST

Forget satellite imagery and Doppler radar — all you really need to forecast the weather is a pig spleen. At least that's all Tomkins' Gus Wickstrom needed. Wickstrom made a name for himself predicting the weather by examining the shape, size, colour and texture of a pig spleen. Then he ate his forecast. Following a Swedish custom, Wickstrom took a bite of the raw spleen to gauge the thickness of the organ — an important factor in rainfall and temperature predictions. Gus Wickstrom died of pneumonia in June 2007.

SUNSHINE

Saskatchewan gets an average 2,206 hours of sunshine per year, more than any other province. In contrast, Newfoundland and Labrador, the least sunny province, sees just 1,563 sun hours annually.

Each year, Saskatchewan residents can expect to see the sun on 310.73 days, considerably more than residents of Nunavut who see the sun on only 268.76 days of the year.

Source: Environment Canada.

GROWING SEASON

In an average year, seeding can begin at the end of April, though progress may be slow until the second week of May. In some years, seeding can continue into the second week of June in northern Saskatchewan. Typically, 90 percent of the most important crops — spring wheat and barley — are reaped by the end of September.

WHEN IT WILL GROW

Moose Jaw	May 20-September 18
Prince Albert	June 2-September 4
Regina	May 21-September 10
Saskatoon	May 21-September 15
Weyburn	May 22-September 12.

Source: TDC Farm Gate.

Take 5 — SASKATCHEWAN'S TOP FIVE EXTREME HOT TEMPERATURES

1. **45.0°C** at Midale and Yellow Grass on July 5,1937.
2. **43.5°C** at Kincaid on June 5,1988.
3. **43.3°C** at Aneroid on June 16,1931 and at Lumsden on July 19,1944.
4. **42.0°C** at Leney on June 5, 1988.
5. **40.5°C** at Cypress Hills on May 29, 1988.

RAIN

In Canada, rain does not fall mainly on the plains — Saskatchewan gets relatively slight amounts of rain. Of Canada's 13 provinces and territories, Saskatchewan comes tenth, recording an annual rainfall of 311.14 mm compared to Nova Scotia's 1081.70 mm.

- Saskatchewan residents only need their umbrellas on 129 days of the year.

Source: Environment Canada.

DUST STORMS

Between 1933 and 1937, Saskatchewan received only 60 percent of its normal rainfall. Coinciding with the Great Depression, the timing could not have been worse. Thousands of head of livestock were lost, crops withered, and 250,000 people abandoned their land to seek better lives elsewhere.

When the soil dried up, the wind picked up, and dust storms swept across the prairies. These storms wreaked more havoc on the struggling prairies, causing soil erosion and vegetation loss. The dust-clogged air even triggered sometimes-fatal respiratory conditions.

WHEN IT RAINS...

In 1953, just 192 mm of rain fell in Saskatchewan. The following year, a Denver, Colorado-based company, Weather Modification Ltd., appeared on the scene, offering to make it rain. The company claimed it could seed clouds and make it rain by shooting a chemical spray into the atmosphere. Whether it was a fluke or the result of science, a whopping 378.3 mm of rain fell in Saskatoon in 1954. Of course too much rain is as bad as too little, and Saskatchewan farmers protested so loudly that Weather Modification Ltd. had to leave town.

Source: Environment Canada; Saskatoon Library.

Take 5 — TOP FIVE SASKATCHEWAN WEATHER WORDS

1. **Grasshopper Blizzards:** During droughts, conditions are ripe for grasshopper infestations. Grasshopper outbreaks, which occur every ten to twelve years and can last for several years, can cause tens of million of dollars in crop damage. When they strike, there are cloudbursts of grasshoppers and the insects cover fields and roads and must even be wiped from car windshields.

2. **Plough Wind:** These straight-line down burst winds come with thunderstorms. These downdrafts rush to the ground with great force, up to 100 to 150 km/h and occasionally even higher. Although the damage from plough winds is usually confined to an area less than three km across, they are known to topple trees, destroy buildings and lift roofs.

3. **Polar Pig:** This is a frigid Arctic air mass that comes squealing in from the north, ushering in a deep freeze.

4. **The Big White Combine:** This is a severe hailstorm that occurs during harvest time, so named because it cuts down crops faster than a combine harvester.

5. **Snow Rollers:** Snow rollers occur when the wind blows wet snow into a rolling ball. Certain conditions – light snowfall, temperatures slightly above freezing and strong winds – must be present. The rolling ball of snow becomes cylindrical, often with a hole through it length-wise. Snow rollers range in size from that of eggs to small barrels.

TOP FIVE EXTREME DAILY RAINFALLS

1. **August 3, 1985:** 380 mm of rain fell on Parkman
2. **July 3, 2000:** 330 mm of rain fell at Vanguard
3. **May 30,1961:** 250 mm fell on Buffalo Gap
4. **June 15,1887:** 160.3 mm fell at Regina
5. **June 27, 1998:** 152 mm fell at Cypress Hills

FLOODED

Despite the prevalence of prairie droughts, Saskatchewan has also been home to devastating floods, usually thanks to springtime snowmelt or severe thunderstorms that spawn torrential rains. Adding to the problem is province's flat, low-level terrain. When waters rise, there is simply no place for it to go and so farmers' fields and streets are submerged.

DÉJA VU ALL OVER AGAIN: WATERS RISE AT RED EARTH

In April 2007, 600 residents of the Red Earth First Nation re-lived a nightmare when they were evacuated from their homes after the flood-prone Carrot River spilled its banks yet again. For the second year in a row, residents were forced to seek refuge in neighbouring communities. Red Earth was not alone. Sixteen other communities all reported severe flooding that required evacuations.

They Said It

"In a just world, sweat and tears might have counted for something in the rain gauge."

– Historian Beth LaDow, on pioneer farmers.

PASS THE SHOVEL

Saskatchewan gets the second least amount of snow of any province or territory in Canada. On average, the province gets 144.98 cm of snow a year – much less than the 451.93 cm that blankets Canada's snowiest place, Newfoundland and Labrador. Only Alberta, which gets 140.41 cm of snow a year, gets less.

Saskatchewan also only gets snowfall on 67 days of the year, compared to the snowiest province, Quebec, where white stuff falls on 109 days.

Snow stays on the Saskatchewan ground for an average 156 days, placing Saskatchewan's length of snow cover in eighth. By comparison, Nunavut has the most days of snow cover at 264.85 days and Nova Scotia has the fewest at 86.96 days a year.

This is not to say that Saskatchewan doesn't get tested by winter. Regina can typically see up to 27 blowing snow days each winter.

Source: Environment Canada.

CH-CH-CHILLY

Saskatchewan may get off relatively easy when it comes to snow, but make no mistake about it: winters can be tough. On average, Saskatchewan experiences 211.58 days a year when temperatures dip below 0°C. In the winter months, the average night time temperature drops to -22.71°C.

Prince Albert is Saskatchewan's coldest city. Compared to 100 other Canadian cities, it comes third for the most days at -20°C or less — Prince Albertans see 66 such days. Meanwhile, Swift Current ranks 13th for extreme wind chill, which can dip to chilly lows of -58.83°C.

Did you know...

that Saskatchewan has more hot days than any province or territory? On seven days of the year the mercury climbs over 30°C.

They Said It

BLIZZARDS

January is notorious for blizzards, which occur most often in the southwestern corner of the province where the storms last an average 12 hours. Both Swift Current and Regina average 30 blizzard hours a year. At Saskatoon, blizzard hours average 6 a year, but a full-fledged four-hour winter blowout only happens once every two years.

Source: Environment Canada.

THE BLIZZARD OF '64

Saskatchewan will not soon forget December 1964. Mid-month, a huge storm created havoc when bone-chilling temperatures of -34°C and winds gusting to 90 km/hr buffeted the province for two days. As a result of the storm's extreme cold, three people died in their homes when their wood stoves went out during the night.

HOW LOW CAN IT GO

When the "feel-like" wind chill temperatures reach dangerous lows that are expected to last three or more hours, Environment Canada issues wind chill warnings. In southern Saskatchewan, it takes wind speeds of 13 km/h or more and a wind chill of -40 or colder for a warning to be issued, and in the north, wind speeds of 13 km/h or more and a wind chill of -45 or colder.

Take 5 SASKATCHEWAN'S TOP FIVE LOWEST TEMPERATURES

1. **-56.7°C**, observed at Prince Albert on February 1, 1893. This is the coldest temperature on record for the province.
2. **-55°C**, at Butte St. Pierre on January 25, 1972.
3. **-52.6°C** at Key Lake on January 29, 2004.
4. **-52.2°C** recorded at La Ronge on February 15, 1936.
5. **-52.0°C** observed at Cote on January 19,1996.

WHITE CHRISTMAS

The chances of having a white Christmas in Saskatchewan vary according to where you are celebrating the holiday. Saskatoon has 98 percent chance of a white Christmas, while Regina has a 93 percent chance. Both have about a 1 in 4 chance of a "perfect" Christmas, with at least 2 cm on the ground and snow in the air.

The greatest snowfall recorded on Christmas day in Saskatoon was 7.6 cm in 1922 and 8.1 cm in Regina in 1975.

PAYING FOR WINTER

The March 2007 figures compiled for winter snow and ice control costs in the province were estimated to be $26.5 million.

Source: Legislative Assembly of Saskatchewan.

Did you know...

that on August 27, 1973, the largest documented hailstone in Canadian history fell in Cedoux, Saskatchewan? The stone weighed in at 290 grams and was 114 mm in diameter.

They Said It

MUD SEASON

It's a running joke that there are five seasons in Saskatchewan: spring, summer, autumn, winter and mud season.

Mud season is caused when the prairies' natural grasses are flattened by winter snow. When the ground thaws and spring rains fall, the prairie soil becomes a thick quagmire, making it very difficult for people to travel off the beaten path. Many Saskatchewanians find themselves isolated until mudded-up roads have a chance to dry up. Farm work is stalled until the ground is solid enough to accommodate tractors and plows.

THE REGINA CYCLONE

June 30, 1912 lives on as a day of infamy in Regina. That day, the deadliest tornado in Canadian history, dubbed the Regina Cyclone, leveled much of the city. The nightmare began at 5 pm. The storm formed 18 km south of the city and by the time it arrived there, it was 400 m wide and had winds of 800 km/h. When the winds subsided after just 20 minutes, 28 people were dead and hundreds injured. As well, 2,500 people were homeless and 500 buildings were damaged or destroyed to the tune of $1,200,000 in damages.

They Said It

WIND

Saskatchewan is not the windiest province in Canada, but its relatively flat landscape does not impede the winds that do blow through. The province's average wind speed of 13.13 km/hr is just slightly below the Canadian average of 14.14 km/hr. Each year, Saskatchewan has 22 windy days — days when winds blow for at least an hour at least 40 km/h. This is many fewer than the 96.63 windy days recorded in Canada's windiest region, Nunavut.

Source: Environment Canada.

WIND POWER

Saskatchewan got its first wind power project, the 17-turbine SunBridge Wind Power Facility in 2002. Nearby is the Cypress Wind Power Facility with 16 turbines. Together these facilities generate enough wind to power 9,000 homes.

In June 2006, the province's wind producing capacity grew with the opening of the Centennial Wind Power Facility. Located near Swift Current, the facility is the largest in Canada. It has 83 turbines and can power 64,000 homes.

Source: Sask Power.

Did you know...

that many Saskatchewan farmers buy hail insurance on their crops? Premiums collected and losses paid each year average $20 million.

LIGHTNING

Southern Saskatchewan is one of the most lightning-prone areas in Canada. Regina gets 113 lightening flashes per 100 km, and Saskatoon, 71. Windsor, ON, the lightning capital of Canada, records 251 flashes and Inuvik, NT, just one.

Source: Environment Canada.

WEATHER OF DEVASTATION

On average, 10 to 15 severe hailstorms inflict devastating blows to Canada's bread basket province each summer, the damage varying with the intensity and the size of the hailstones. Most hail is pea-sized, but every so often hail the size of oranges and grapefruit pummel the province.

NOT THE FOGGIEST

Saskatchewan's inland location means the province gets little fog. The province contends with fog on just 22.73 days a year, compared to the foggiest province, Nova Scotia, which is fogged in 81.63 days.

Source: Environment Canada.

Weblinks

Weather Winners

www.on.ec.gc.ca/weather/winners/intro-e.html

See how your hometown or province stacks up to others across our vast nation on the topic of weather. To claim bragging rights on such issues as sunniest, driest, and wettest weather go to this site.

Road Information

roadinfo.telenium.ca/shwyw.html

This site offers an on-line up-to-date report on road conditions and how they are affected by the weather.

The Regina Cyclone

http://library2.usask.ca/sni/stories/con19.html

One of the worst weather disasters in the province's history, the memory of the 1912 Regina Cyclone remains etched in the collective memory of the city and province. Find out more about this weather event at this page maintained by the University of Saskatchewan Library.

Pig Spleen Forecasting

www.almanac.com/weathercenter/pigspleen.php

See how Gus did it! Your guide to forecasting the weather, pig spleen style.

Crime and Punishment

CRIME LINE

1873: The Canadian Parliament decides to establish a Mounted Police Force for the Northwest Territories. A year later, 300 members of the North West Mounted Police (NWMP) move to what is now Saskatchewan and Alberta.

1885: In the spring, disgruntled Métis begin an uprising in an effort to protect their land and way of life. The final skirmish between the Métis and federal forces happens on May 9 at the community of Batoche. Canadian forces win, the uprising is quashed, and Louis Riel is arrested and charged with treason.

1885: On November 16, Louis Riel is hanged in Regina.

1892: The Regina Police Service is created.

1907: Robert E. Dunning is appointed the first Chief of Police in Saskatoon.

1908: A jail is built in Moosomin.

1910: The first rules and regulations of the Saskatoon Police Department are approved.

1910: On February 17, the province of Saskatchewan's first death sentence is carried out. Regina's Santford Hainer is executed.

1915: A jail opens in Regina.

Big Muddy

The Big Muddy badlands of south western Saskatchewan typified the untamed "Wild West." This area of canyons and gulches straddles the US border and provided excellent hiding places for horse thieves, cattle rustlers and outlaws in the late 19th and early 20th centuries.

A number of outlaws earned their reputations in the Big Muddy.

Nova Scotia-born outlaw Sam Kelley, AKA Charles 'Red' Nelson, was one half of the notorious Nelson-Jones Gang, and one of the wild west's most wanted men. With his partner Frank Jones, the duo specialized in horse and cattle theft and bank and train robberies.

When Kelley and his crew were forced to flee to Canada – a frequent occurrence – they found refuge in a series of caves just over the border. Large enough to shelter and conceal the outlaws and their horses, these hideouts, located on a rise of land, provided an eagle eye view of the surrounding territory.

By 1902, Kelley was tired of being on the lam and turned himself in to Montanan authorities. Lacking evidence, the state had no choice but to acquit him. Then Kelley left his life of crime. Around 1909 he purchased a ranch in the Big Muddy Valley. Four years later he moved to Debden, 75 kilometres northwest of Prince Albert. Kelley was apparently a well-behaved homesteader and lived his final years far from the excitement of outlaw life. In 1937, a hungry and confused Kelley was found in Smeaton, Saskatchewan. He was committed to a hospital where he died.

1915: In July, the Saskatchewan government abolishes all bar liquor licenses and takes over the wholesale of alcohol, making Saskatchewan the first province in Canada to ban private sector sales of booze.

1921: A jail is opened in Prince Albert.

1925: The Saskatchewan government abandons prohibition, but continues to control wholesale outlets for selling and distributing alcohol.

1935: On July 1, the RCMP attempt to arrest On-to-Ottawa trek leaders sparking the Regina Riot that saw the deaths of one police officer and one trekker.

Saskatchewan's Little Chicago

Moose Jaw was once thought of as a quiet, sleepy city. That was until 1985, when a truck fell through a downtown street, revealing a vast network of underground tunnels rumoured to have been the site of shady dealings during the years of American prohibition. Earning the nickname "Little Chicago," Moose Jaw was home to a distribution route that fed booze to thirsty Minneapolis and Chicago between 1919 and 1933.

According to local folklore, this bootlegging industry was controlled by legendary Chicago gangster, Al Capone, who is rumoured to have operated the gambling dens and brothels along River Street that were connected by the underground tunnel.

There is tantalizing evidence of Capone's Saskatchewan life. Barbers and physicians claim to have offered their services to the infamous outlaw and Regina court documents show that Capone was nearly sued for shipping 60 cases of bad liquor; the suit was withdrawn when Capone refunded the money. Another shred of evidence is a dental appointment book containing the name "Al Brown" — a known Capone alias.

1946: On February 20, Saskatchewan's last death sentence is carried out when 20-year-old Jack Loran is hanged in Regina, convicted on a charge of robbery.

1946: On March 1, the province appoints a Saskatchewan Penal Commission to examine all aspects of the province's punitive system. In September the Commission's report is released, recommending a vast overhaul.

1967: At Shell Lake, James and Evelyn Peterson and seven of their eight children living at home are shot and killed by Victor Ernest Hoffman, who uses a .22-calibre Belgian Browning pump-action repeater rifle at close range. Hoffman is arrested by the RCMP four days later.

1968: Victor Ernest Hoffman is found not guilty for the Peterson murders by reason of insanity.

1969: On New Year's Eve, Gail Miller, a 20-year-old nursing aide, is found dead in a Saskatoon snow bank.

1969: Sixteen-year-old David Milgaard is arrested on May 30 and charged with the murder of Gail Miller.

1970: A year to the day that Gail Miller was found dead, Milgaard, who had been convicted of the crime, is sentenced to life in prison.

1971: On January 31, Milgaard's appeal is rejected by the Saskatchewan Court of Appeal. In November, another appeal is refused by the Supreme Court of Canada.

1981: Correctional facilities open in Prince Albert and Saskatoon.

The Wrong Man:
The David Milgaard Case

Imagine spending 23 years in jail for a crime you didn't commit. That's exactly what happened to David Milgaard. In 1969, Milgaard, who was just 16, was hitchhiking across the country with two friends. A stop in Saskatoon on January 31st would forever change his life. That same day, Gail Miller, a 20-year-old nursing aid, was raped and murdered. Four months later, the young Milgaard was arrested, charged in her death.

The evidence in Milgaard's case was circumstantial. Milgaard had the same blood type as the murderer. As well, the teenager had coincidentally visited the evidence-laden home of the killer while in Saskatoon. Milgaard's fate was further sealed by his young traveling companions who were pressured by police to testify against their pal. Eventually, one of the friends testified he had actually witnessed Milgaard stab Gail. Exactly one year after Miller's murder, 17-year-old David Milgaard was sentenced to life imprisonment. Milgaard never wavered in maintaining his innocence even though his refusal to admit guilt cost him several parole opportunities.

Luckily for Milgaard, his mother, Joyce, believed her son. Her faith in him would win his release. Undaunted by her son's sentence, Joyce hired her own legal team – and its investigation forced the case to be reopened.

In 1992, the Supreme Court of Canada recommended a new trial. The province of Saskatchewan decided not to prosecute him again, and he was formally acquitted. Joyce nevertheless remained committed to prove her son's innocence.

In 1997, DNA tests proved that Milgaard had not committed the murder and showed that serial rapist Larry Fisher was the assailant. Fisher was arrested in Calgary and in 1999 was convicted in the murder of Gail Miller and sentenced to life in prison.

Milgaard has received an apology from the Saskatchewan government and $10 million in compensation.

1981: In May, Colin Thatcher's ex-wife, JoAnn Wilson, survives being shot in the shoulder after someone fires a high-powered rifle through her kitchen window in Regina.

1983: On January 21, JoAnne Wilson is found dead in the garage of her Regina home. Colin Thatcher is charged with murder.

1984: In October, Colin Thatcher's murder trial begins. It wraps with his conviction on November 6.

1988: David Milgaard's lawyers apply to have his case reopened.

1990: Federal Justice Minister Kim Campbell ignores David Milgaard's mother, Joyce, when she tries to give the minister a forensic report that could clear her son. Campbell claims that looking at the report would risk any future review of the case.

1990: On November 25, Neil Stonechild, a young Native man, dies of hypothermia after being dropped off on the outskirts of Saskatoon by police. His body is found four days later.

1991: Justice Minister Kim Campbell turns down David Milgaard's request for a case review. In August, his lawyers try again and in November Minister Campbell orders the Supreme Court to review Milgaard's conviction.

1991: On April 14, the Supreme Court rules that Milgaard should have a new trial. Saskatchewan decides not to prosecute Milgaard again and he is freed, but not formally acquitted.

1993: On October 24, farmer Robert Latimer kills his 12-year old daughter Tracy in what he says was an act of mercy for the severely disabled girl.

1994: A jury convicts Robert Latimer of second degree murder in the killing of his daughter.

1996: Serial killer John Crawford is convicted of the murders of three First Nations women.

1997: In February the Supreme Court orders a new trial for Robert Latimer, which begins on October.

Take 5 — CARMEN HARRY'S TOP FIVE INTERESTING FACTS

ABOUT THE SASKATCHEWAN RCMP

Carmen Harry is the curator of RCMP historical collections unit. She was born and raised in Mexico and worked for several National Museums and the National Capital Commission in Ottawa, before working for the RCMP Centennial Museum and now the RCMP Historical Collections Unit located at the new RCMP Heritage Centre.

1. **Establishing an HQ** - The North West Mounted Police established its headquarters in Regina in the fall of 1882 remaining there until 1920 when the Mounted Police became a Federal Police and moved its Headquarters to Ottawa.

2. **Saying Goodbye** - Roche Percée (near Estevan) was the place where all of the members of the North West Mounted Police were all together for the last time.

3. **Training Grounds** - The RCMP "Depot" Division, the training centre for all the members of the Mounted Police was established November 1, 1885 in Regina.

4. **The Biggest of the Bunch** - The RCMP Academy is the largest of RCMP establishments with 52 buildings located on 740 acres of land in Regina.

5. **The Oldest** - The RCMP Chapel, located at "Depot" Division in Regina, was built in 1883 by John Ross. It is the oldest standing building in Regina.

1997: In July, DNA evidence proves David Milgaard's innocence. The government of Saskatchewan apologizes for his wrongful imprisonment.

1997: On July 25, Larry Fisher is arrested in Calgary for Gail Miller's murder.

1997: In November Robert Latimer is again found guilty. The jury recommends he be eligible for parole after one year.

1997: The judge in the Latimer case gives the convicted "constitutional exemption," and orders a sentence of less than two years, with one of these to be spent in the community.

1998: The Saskatchewan Court of Appeal sets aside Latimer's constitutional exemption and upholds the mandatory minimum sentence of 10 years.

1990: Latimer appeals his case to the Supreme Court of Canada. In June the Supreme Courts hears his appeal.

1999: The Milgaard family receives a $10 million compensation package from the federal government.

1999: The Fisher trial begins in Yorkton. The trial is not held in Saskatoon because of potential juror bias there. Fisher is convicted of murdering Gail Miller and is later sentenced to life in prison.

2001: Victor Ernest Hoffman, who committed the Peterson murders, dies of cancer.

2001: The Supreme Court of Canada upholds Robert Latimer's sentence of life in prison with no chance for parole for 10 years.

2001: A task group is formed to develop a strategy that will reduce the number of motor vehicle thefts in Regina.

2004: The provincial government releases a report, noting there was clear evidence Stonechild had been in police custody the night of his death. The following month, two Saskatoon officers are fired from the police force in connection to the Stonechild case.

2006: In November, Colin Thatcher is granted full parole and released from prison.

2010: Thirty-four-year-old Brendan William Cross of Regina was charged with indecency, assault and uttering threats after trying to get into the office of Regina mayor, Pat Fiacco. He made the visit in a partial birthday suit, naked from the waist down.

Neil Stonechild

Relations between Aboriginals and Saskatoon city police have long been strained. They got worse in 1990 when, on November 23, 17-year-old Neil Stonechild, a young First Nation's man, was found partially clothed, frozen to death on the outskirts of town.

His death was ruled accidental, but the First Nations community believed Stonechild was the victim of a long standing practice whereby police abandoned First Nation's men at the edge of town during winter months. Outraged, they called for an investigation. Their calls fell on deaf ears.

Thirteen years later, following the freezing deaths of three more Native men and in the wake of allegations by Darrell Night that he had been forced from a police cruiser outside of town in the dead of winter, the Saskatchewan government agreed to the long-demanded investigation. The 2004 report was shocking. It revealed that Stonechild had indeed been in police custody the night of his death.

The two officers accused in the Stonechild case still maintain they had no contact with the teen on that night, but two other officers were charged with unlawful confinement in connection with the Darryl Night case and were fired from the force. The force acknowledged it was guilty of this heinous practice. Said Police Chief Russell Sabo, "I think we have to take ownership of things that have transpired. It happened more than once and we fully admit that and, in fact, on behalf of the police department I want to apologize to those people who we had said it was a one-of-a-kind incident."

THE HOME OF CANADA'S POLICE FORCE

Saskatchewan was long the headquarters of the North-West Mounted Police. The force arrived in 1874 and, after several attempts to establish a permanent head quarters, Wascana Creek, on the outskirts of Regina, became its home in 1882.

In 1904, the force had "Royal" added to its title, a gesture of thanks from King Edward VII for the force's participation in the South African Boer War.

Saskatchewan remained the home of the force until 1920. That year the RNWMP moved to Ottawa, and renamed the Royal Canadian Mounted Police (RCMP), and charged with federally policing the whole of Canada.

Although Regina is no longer the home to RCMP headquarters, it is still home to the RCMP Academy, and has been so for over 120 years. All RCMP officers across Canada start their careers in Regina where they receive basic training.

PROHIBITION

Following World War One, a North American-wide movement to ban liquor began. In April 1915, Saskatchewan Liberal Premier Walter Scott cracked down on bars and they were ordered to close by 7 p.m. That July, the government got tougher, abolishing all bar liquor licenses and taking over the wholesale of alcohol. Saskatchewan thus became the first province to ban private sector sales of booze (all provinces but Quebec would follow by 1917). Saskatchewan bar owners demanded compensation for lost of revenues, but their complaints fell on deaf ears. In 1918, the federal government got in on the prohi-

Did you know...

that the first female RCMP officer was admitted to the force in 1974?

bition fun and banned the manufacture, importation and transportation of beverages containing more than 2.5 per cent alcohol.

Saskatchewanians are a resourceful bunch, however, and despite the ban, people found ways to drink. In rural areas, backyard stills bubbled and percolated. Indeed a booming elicit booze trade lined many peoples' pockets.

By 1919, the Canada Temperance Act replaced prohibition as public opinion shifted in favour of decriminalized alcohol consumption. In 1925, the Saskatchewan government abandoned prohibition by instituting a system of government-controlled outlets for selling and distributing alcohol.

CRIME IN SASKATCHEWAN

- Rate of criminal code incidents (per 100,000 people) recorded in Saskatchewan annually: 14,320
- Rate of criminal code incidents recorded in all of Canada annually: 7,761

Source: Government of Saskatchewan; Statistics Canada.

CRIMES IN SASKATCHEWAN (AND IN CANADA)

- 142,354 criminal code incidents (2.5 million)
- 43 homicides (658)
- 16,163 assaults (234,729)
- 1,243 robberies (28,669)
- 6,177 motor vehicle thefts (160,100)
- 14,596 break-and-enters (259,521)
- 1,307 sexual assaults (23,303)
- 30,145 mischief cases (353,955)

VIOLENT CRIME

The rate of violent crime in Saskatchewan, 1,983 per 100,000 population, more than doubles the national rate of 943 per 100,000. It is greater than the Quebec rate of 739, but far less than the rate in Nunavut, 7,042 per 100,000.

PROPERTY CRIME

- Rate of property crime in Saskatchewan: 5,484 per 100,000
- National rate: 3,738 per 100,000
- Rate in Newfoundland and Labrador, the lowest: 2,535 per 100,000
- Rate in the Northwest Territories, the highest: 6,484 per 100,000

DRUG CRIME

In 2003, 778 people were convicted of drug related offences in Saskatchewan. Of those, 503 people were picked up for possessing drugs, while 275 were picked up for trying to sell drugs.

Source: RCMP.

MOTOR VEHICLE THEFT

Saskatchewan ranks third in Canada for motor vehicle theft. Each day 550 automobile thefts per 100,000 population are recorded. Only Manitoba (1,148) and BC (812) have more.

In 2000, Regina had the highest rate of automobile theft of any North American city. The 1,594 cars stolen per 100,000 population was greater than the rate of car thefts of all major cities in North America, including Los Angeles and New York. There is a silver lining, however. Ninety six percent of Regina's stolen cars are returned.

Source: Statistics Canada.

YOUTH CRIME

- Saskatchewan has the dubious distinction of having the highest incidence of youth crime in Canada. While the national rate of youth crime (per 100,000 people) stood at 3 percent in 2006, Saskatchewan's rate hit 7 percent.
- In 2005, 18,563 crimes were committed by youth in Saskatchewan per 100,000. It is the highest youth crime rate in Canada, followed by Manitoba and Nova Scotia.
- The national youth crime rate in 2005 was 6,603 per 100,000.

Sources: Canadian Centre for Justice Statistics; Government of Saskatchewan.

URBAN CRIME RATE

The Regina CMA crime rate fell by 8 percent and the Saskatoon CMA rate was down 9 percent in 2006. The 2006 Regina CMA crime rate was 12,415 *Criminal Code* incidents per 100,000 population and the Saskatoon rate was 12,209.

- Murder rate (per 100,000 people) in Regina: 4.0
- Murder rate in Saskatoon 3.7
- Robbery rate in Regina: 197
- Robbery rate in Saskatoon: 248
- Break-in rate in Regina, the highest in Canada: 1,740
- Break-in rate in Saskatoon, the second highest in Canada: 1,494
- Motor vehicle theft rate in Regina: 1,078
- Motor vehicle theft rate in Saskatoon: 550

Source: Statistics Canada.

COLIN THATCHER AND JOANN WILSON

It was January 21, 1983 and JoAnn Wilson was getting out of her car in her garage when she was grabbed from behind. She was bludgeoned, brought to her knees by blows from a heavy instrument. When Wilson tried to escape, her assailant shot her with a handgun.

JoAnn Wilson's death came as a shock to the city of Regina. The respected woman was a member of the city's upper crust. A fifteen month investigation followed her death. As weeks slipped by, police began to form their case. The accused was none other Wilson's ex-husband, Colin Thatcher, a man who had at one time been Saskatchewan's Minister of Energy and Mines.

A media circus surrounded the case. In November 1984, Thatcher was convicted of first-degree murder and sentenced to life in prison – the first government minister ever to be convicted of murder.

Thatcher served his sentence at an Edmonton maximum security prison until 1998, when he moved to the Ferndale minimum-security facility near Mission, BC. In 2006, a storm of controversy erupted when Thatcher was granted full parole and released from prison.

Take 5 TOP FIVE CRIMES COMMITTED IN SASKATCHEWAN

1. Mischief
2. Theft under and over $5,000
3. Assault
4. Break-and-enters
5. Motor vehicle thefts

FAKIN' IT

- In 2008, the number of counterfeit bank notes passed in Saskatchewan: 1,112
- Number of fake notes seized by police in Saskatchewan: 999 (47 percent)
- Number passed nationally in the same year: 232,511
- Number seized nationally: 35,395 (46.3 percent)

Source: RCMP.

STOLEN IDENTITY

In the latest available data, 94 Saskatchewanians complained of stolen identities. It cost them $61,192.28. Nationally, there were a total of 7,778 complaints of ID theft, which cost Canadians over $16 million.

Source: Canadian Anti-fraud Call Centre.

TAKING A BITE OUT OF CRIME

Since 1987, Crime Stoppers has helped take a bite out of Saskatchewan crime. Since the organization's inception 20 years ago, the group has been instrumental in solving 3,061 cases, arresting 2,633 offenders, recovering over $7 million in property and confiscating nearly $7 million in drugs.

They Said It

TO SERVE AND PROTECT

- Number of police officers in Saskatchewan: 2,030
- Number in Canada: 62,458
- Number per 100,000 citizens in Saskatchewan: 205
- Number per 100,000 citizens in Canada: 192

THE MUSICAL RIDE

There is nothing more quintessentially Canadian than the Canadian Mountie. And nowhere does the Mountie shine more brightly than in the world-famous musical ride, a tradition rooted in Saskatchewan.

The Musical Ride was developed by the early North-West Mounted Police in order to display their horse riding agility and to entertain western outposts. It has been said that the Musical Ride was performed as early as 1876, but the first officially recorded performance happened at the Regina Barracks in 1887. It was first publicly performed in 1901.

Today the musical ride remains a Canadian icon. Members of the Ride, all of whom have been RCMP officers for at least two years, volunteer for the opportunity to participate and undergo months and months of grueling equestrian training to do so. Each member can ride for three years.

Today's troop consists of 32 riders and horses, plus a member in charge of precision drills set to music. The highlight of each performance is undoubtedly the charge. In this impressive maneuver, each rider lowers his or her lance, with red and white pennons, and prompt their horses to gallop.

DOING TIME
- Number of adults admitted to correctional facilities annually, according to the latest available data: 9,026
- Number of adults given probation and conditional sentences: 4,969
- Number of youths admitted to correctional facilities: 234
- Number of youths given probation and community service: 1,381
- Incarceration rate for youth in Saskatchewan per 10,000 youth: 25.69

INCARCERATION
Almost a quarter of the 15,912 people convicted in Saskatchewan annually do time for their crimes while another 9.5 percent receive a conditional sentence, acccording to the latest data. Thirty-one percent of those found guilty were given probation. In Canada, the same year saw 257,127 convicted with 35 percent being incarcerated, 5.2 percent receiving a conditional sentence and 46 percent receive probation.
- Adult incarceration rate in Saskatchewan (per 100,000): 160
- The rate in Nova Scotia, the lowest in Canada: 42
- The national rate: 129
- Probation rate in Saskatchewan: 542
- Probation rate in Canada: 396

AVERAGE JOE OFFENDER
- The average age of offenders in Saskatchewan: 30
- Percentage of offenders who end up in jail: 24
- Average sentence: 92 days

Did you know...

that Musical Ride horses begin their training at three years of age and begin Musical Ride training when they are six years old?

Weblinks

Saskatchewan Crime Rates
www.statcan.ca/Daily/English/050721/d050721a.htm
Want to see how Saskatchewan stacks up, crime wise? Have a look at this Statistics Canada website featuring a neat little table of 2005 statistics on many crime measurements by province and territory.

Royal Canadian Mounted Police
www.rcmp-grc.gc.ca/sk/index_e.htm
Visit this site to find out what the RCMP are up to in Saskatchewan. Here you can see the organization's priorities, plans and programs for preventing crime in the province.

Crime Stoppers of Saskatchewan
www.saskcrimestoppers.com
Stay current with the unsolved crime of the week.

Culture

The culture of Saskatchewan is diverse. It is multicultural, celebrating the traditions of the First People and a host of newcomers from around the world. It incorporates the cheatin' and lovin' songs of Country and Western, but is firmly rooted in other musical genres as well, and notably lays claim to famed folk-rocker Joni Mitchell. Saskatchewan is also a cultural hotbed for Canadian literature, film and TV – more and more of it, from TV's "Corner Gas" to Guy Vanderhaeghe's epic novels, are set here, giving Saskatchewan a place in the Canadian consciousness.

ARTISTS
- Number of artists in Canada: 131,000
- Number in Saskatchewan: 2,970
- Percentage of these who live in Regina or Saskatoon: 62

THAT'S AN ORDER
- Saskatchewan recipients of the Order of Canada: 181
- Members of the order: 172
- Officers of the order: 1
- Companions of the order: 7
- David Ahenakew was stripped of the Order of Canada on July 11, 2005 for anti-Semitic comments.

IN ORDER

The Saskatchewan Order of Merit has been awarded to 137 residents of Saskatchewan. This highest provincial honour recognizes citizens who have displayed excellence and have positively influenced the province. Recipients receive an insignia shaped like a western lily (the provincial flower) and stamped with the Crown and Shield of Arms of the province, suspended from a ribbon of green and gold, the province's official colours. The prize is awarded by the Lieutenant Governor in an autumn investiture ceremony that alternates between Regina and Saskatoon. Members of the Order are permitted to use the post-nominal letters S.O.M.

THE ARTS

In 2009, the Canada Council for the Arts granted $3.5 million to the arts in Saskatchewan, 2.61 percent of the Council's national funding. Saskatchewan's arts funding, which amounts to $720 per person, is the 6th highest in Canada.

The largest amount of funding went to visual arts in the amount of $1.2 million. Theatre received the second largest amount of funding at $748,330, followed by writing and publishing with $584,205.

Regina received $1.77 million, or 48.1 percent of all funding granted in the province. Saskatoon received 44 percent, or $1.55 million in funds. In all, 14 other communities received $203,994, or 5.8 percent of all funding.

Source: Canada Council for the Arts.

Did you know...

that Saskatchewan has produced 425 NHLers, more than any other province?

Bio THE ENGLISHMAN'S BOY

Born in the mining and farming town of Esterhazy in 1951, Guy Vanderhaeghe has become that most curious of things in Saskatchewan, an actual writer who earns his keep from his pen. He is a bona fide CanLit star, but carries himself with typical Saskatchewan modesty.

Like most writers, his was a circuitous route. He had studied history at the University of Saskatchewan. For a time he worked as an archivist and later, as a teacher. In the late 1970s, a life altering experience – a diagnosis of diabetes at age 26 – called his bluff, and he's been writing ever since.

His first book, a collection of short stories titled *Man Descending* (1980) won rave international acclaim and both the UK-based Faber prize and the Governor General's Award in 1982. Two more short story collections followed: *The Trouble with Heroes* (1983) and *Things as They Are?* (1992).

He published his first novel, *My Present Age*, in 1984, and in1989, the novel Homesick won the City of Toronto Book Award. In 1996, Vanderhaeghe won the Governor General's Award again with *The Englishman's Boy*. Considered his most accomplished work to date, it is set in both 1920s Hollywood and in southern Saskatchewan at the time of the 1873 Cypress Hills massacre of Assiniboia First Nations.

His follow up novel, *The Last Crossing* (2001) has likewise garnered strong praise. Also set in the 19th century west, *The Last Crossing* won the CBC's 2004 Canada Reads contest which named Vanderhaeghe's book as one all Canadians should read. Vanderhaeghe's work will also soon be seen on the small screen; the filming of a CBC miniseries version of The Englishman's Boy was completed in 2007.

Vanderhaeghe's work has been characterized by a profound engagement in the history of the province, and he has brought the province and its past to life for readers across the country and around the world. In 2003, Vanderhaeghe was awarded both the Order of Merit and was made an Officer of the Order of Canada.

ARTS SPENDING

- Amount spent on cultural goods annually: 740 million
- Percentage of total consumer spending this accounts for: 3.5
- Average per capita cultural spending in Canada: $821
- The per capita cultural spending in Saskatchewan: $837
- Percentage of Saskatchewan households that spent money on the performing arts in 2005: 38
- Amount these households spent: $26 million
- Percentage of Saskatchewan households that spent money on live sports events in 2005: 32
- Amount these sports fans spent: $25 million

Sources: Canadian Council for the Arts; Hill Strategies Research Inc.

FILM INDUSTRY

"Corner Gas," the hit comedy by Tisdale, Saskatchewan native Brent Butt, is one of the most successful television series ever made in Canada. It, along with with "Little Mosque on the Prairie," has made the Sasktachewan landscape and sensibility familiar to a new generation of Canadians.

The value of the Saskatchewan film and television industry in 2009 is now at $62 million. Forty individual film and television productions entered principal photography in 2008/2009.

Source: SaskFilm and Video Development Corporation.

MOVIE BUSINESS
- Number of movie theatres in Saskatchewan: 40
- Movie admissions collected at theatres: $2.25 million
- Attendance at movie theatres: 3.36 million
- Number of drive-ins: 7
- Number of video stores: 186

LIVE THEATRE
- Number of theatre companies in Saskatchewan: 6
- Number of theatre performances produced annually: 468
- Number of Saskatchewanians who attend live theatre in annually: 106,428
- Revenue generated from these performances: $3.64 million

Source: Statistics Canada.

SHAKESPEARE ON THE SASKATCHEWAN
Beneath the red and white tents nestled along the South Saskatchewan each summer rests one of the province's cultural staples – Shakespeare on the Saskatchewan, a festival which runs in July and August. This annual festival, in its 26th season in 2010, offers two of the bard's plays on the main stage, plus medieval feasts, tours, art displays and the famous Sir Toby's Tavern.

The festival's ensemble of actors is centred on a core of six to seven regulars, with additional professionals and apprentices hired each year to complete the company. Planning and preparation for a season takes approximately three years.

HURRY HARD: THE PROVINCIAL SPORT
Curling has thrived in Saskatchewan since its arrival in 1879. The sport became especially popular in the first decades of the 20th century when special bonspiels, such as "smokers" featuring variety shows and imported cigars, and "carspiels," which offered automobiles as prizes, attracted players.

They Said It

Women have been prominent in the game and Saskatchewan has produced many female curling champions. In 1960, Joyce McKee, Sylvia Fedoruk, Donna Belding and Muriel Coben won the first Canadian women's championship. And of course, one of Saskatchewan's most decorated curling teams of all time was led by Sandra Schmirler supported by Jan Betker, Joan McCusker and Marcia Gudereit. The most accomplished women's team in history, the Schmirler rink earned national and world titles in 1993, 1994 and 1997 and the gold medal at the 1998 Winter Olympics. Curlers and non-curlers alike were devastated when Schmirler, just 36, died of cancer in 2000.

Today, the Saskatchewan Curling Association boasts more than 200 registered clubs, 35,724 members and operates 669 artificial and 32 natural sheets of ice.

They Said It

Did you know...

that Saskatchewan has more golfers per capita than anywhere in the world? Thirty-three percent of Saskatchewan residents over the age of 12 play six or more rounds of golf each year.

Bio PAINTER TURNED SINGER

Joni Mitchell first found stardom with her folk music in the late '60s, but it was in 2000 that Mitchell's fans caught a glimpse of another passion. "Voices: The Work of Joni Mitchell" displayed Mitchell's artwork for the first time in Canada, appropriately in her hometown of Saskatoon. Mitchell has called herself a "painter derailed by circumstance," this circumstance perhaps being her lacking "stick-to-it-iveness"(as suggested by her mother) . . . or just maybe an uninspiring series of college art courses. Whatever the case, it mostly has to do with the fact that Joni Mitchell was extraordinarily gifted as a singer and songwriter.

Roberta Joan Anderson was born in Alberta, but moved to Saskatoon where her father was a grocer and mother a teacher. As a young woman, Joni spent time at Art college, but soon found herself in Toronto pursuing a career in folk music. Soon after, she married folksinger Chuck Mitchell and during their two-year marriage the couple toured as a duo. In 1967, newly divorced, Mitchell moved again, first to New York and then California. There she found solo success as a singer and songwriter.

In 1968, she released her first of 25 successful albums which have featured such hits as "Both Sides Now," "Big Yellow Taxi" and "Help Me." She found fans in the likes of Bob Dylan, Leonard Cohen and Van Morrison, and many artists have recorded her songs.

Mitchell won Grammy Awards for best folk performance in 1969 with Clouds and in 1994 for best pop album with Turbulent Indigo, and received Juno Awards in 1975 for best female vocalist and 2001 for best vocal jazz album. She was inducted into the Juno Hall of Fame in 1981, was the first Canadian woman inducted into the U.S. Rock and Roll Hall of Fame (1997) and received the Grammy Lifetime Achievement Award in 2002. Mitchell is a Companion of the Order of Canada and has her own star on Canada's Walk of Fame.

She continues to be honoured in her home province, notably as one of the featured guests at the Saskatchewan Centennial Gala in 2005 and as the subject of "The Amazing Childhood of Joni Mitchell," a collection of memorabilia from Mitchell's youth, displayed in Saskatoon's Mendel Art Gallery in 2006.

MUSEUMS AND GALLERIES

About one third (32.4 percent) of Saskatchewan residents visited a museum in 1998 – a fourth place finish in Canada. With 269 museums, Saskatchewan ranks first in Canada in terms of the number of heritage institutions per capita.

One in five Saskatchewan residents visits an art gallery each year. The province's art gallery attendance rate of 22.3 percent gives the province another fourth place standing.

Sources: Statistics Canada; Canadian Council for the Arts.

Take 5 FIVE SASKATCHEWAN MUSIC FESTIVALS

1. **Craven Country Jamboree:** Craven Country Jamboree happens in the beautiful Qu'Appelle Valley just north of Regina. Past acts include Tim McGraw, Randy Travis and Tanya Tucker.

2. **Regina Folk Festival:** The Regina Folk Festival has presented a wide variety of musical styles including: old country, bluegrass, operatic rock, Latino, singes, songwriters, roots and blues, Celtic, funk, reggae and jazz.

3. **SaskTel Saskatchewan Jazz Festival:** The SaskTel Saskatchewan Jazz Festival, which features the best of jazz and blues music, is held in Saskatoon, Saskatchewan the last two weeks of June.

4. **Mid-Winter Blues Festival:** Showcasing some of Saskatchewan's best blues talent, the Mid-Winter Blues Festival has continued to grow since its inception.

5. **Ness Creek Music Festival:** Celebrating music, art, ecology and culture in Northern Saskatchewan with four days of workshops, performances and demonstrations for the entire family.

Bio WHO HAS SEEN THE WIND

Perhaps no Canadian writer, past or present, has earned more national fame than Saskatchewan's own William Ormond Mitchell. His folksy takes of western Canadian life have brought to life the rural Saskatchewan world he knew as a child.

Born in Saskatchewan in 1914, W.O. Mitchell lived in Weyburn, SK until a brush with tuberculosis at the age of 12 took his family to Florida, where the climate restored his health. Mitchell returned to Canada in 1931. After a brief recurrence of his illness, Mitchell vowed to pursue his love of writing. In 1940, he enrolled in university where he earned a BA, a teaching certificate and met his wife, Merna Hirtle. In 1944, Mitchell and his family settled in Alberta, but in his heart – and in his writing – he remained close to his Saskatchewan home.

His 1947 *Who has Seen the Wind* was wildly successful, readers seeing in it dark childhood truths and the essence of life on Saskatchewan's prairies. By fictionalizing his hometown of Weyburn in the prairie town of Crocus, Mitchell captured for his readers his beloved home province. This novel was so popular that in 1977 it became a feature film. Numerous novels followed over the next three decades. Though successful in their own rights, none were as enthusiastically greeted as his first.

Mitchell also made his mark as a playwright. His most successful was *Jake and the Kid*. Originally written for *Maclean's*, it became a weekly CBC radio series from 1950-56 and was televised in 1961. He later parlayed the characters from these stories into *According to Jake and the Kid* (1989) which won the Stephen Leacock award for humour. Other accolades followed. He was a Member of the Order of Canada, an honorary Member of the Privy Council and has several honorary degrees.

When W.O Mitchell died in 1998, Rex Murphy noted this of his massive talent, "He will be remembered as a lecturer, performer, stage raconteur, friend of a legion of fledgling writers, . . . a 'presence' in the life and minds of Canadians."

Take 5 TOP FIVE COOL "BIG THINGS" IN SASKATCHEWAN

1. **Mac the Moose in Moose Jaw:** 9.8 m
2. **Lesia the Ukrainian Girl in Canora:** 7.6 m
3. **Santa Claus in Watson:** 6 m
4. **Grasshopper in Wilkie:** 5.5 m
5. **Gopher in Eston:** 2.4 m

GAINER THE GOPHER

Ask anyone from age eight to 88 who Gainer the Gopher is and they'll tell you the six-foot-something, fun-loving gopher is the mascot of the Saskatchewan Roughriders Canadian Football League team. Gainer doesn't speak because, of course, Gophers can't talk. Still, he makes himself known.

Gainer loves his job and engages fans from the sidelines. His animated antics, O-fence and D-fence signs and his infamous butt-wiggling dance have earned him legions of fans. When the Riders score, he proudly perches on his gopher hole and rides up and down the sides of the field. At times, cheers for Gainer outstrip applause for the team itself.

LITERATURE

Governor General's Literary Award winners from Saskatchewan

- 2003: Tim Lilburn, *Kill-site*
- 2003: Allen Sapp, *The Song Within My Heart*
- 2001: Arthur Slade, *Dust*
- 1996: Guy Vanderhaeghe, *The Englishman's Boy*

Did you know...

that NBA All-Star Steve Nash lived in Regina as a toddler for a period of time?

Take 5 BRAD JOHNER'S TOP FIVE FAVOURITE THINGS ABOUT SASKATCHEWAN

A staple of country music radio and video, Brad Johner is no stranger to the Canadian music scene. He's a four-time Juno nominee, a multiple Canadian Country Music Awards winner, and one of Canada's most respected and sought-after performers.

1. **Telemiracle** - It's been a staple in the province for 31 years and I've been a part of the national cast for 10 of those. It's such a great cause, and this year the people of Saskatchewan made donations to the total sum of $5.6 million. Every penny stays in the province to help those who need it most.

2. **Craven Big Valley Jambouree** - Craven is a great get together for Saskatchewan people to share good times in music and fellowship. Not only is it host to some of the biggest international names in country music, but it also showcases great Saskatchewan talent. It's a show for all ages and is a great time.

3. **Corner Gas** - The hit T.V. show is filmed in Saskatchewan, and it really embraces the unique and funny things about life here on the prairies.

4. **Fishing**- There's nothing like fishing on one of the hundred thousand lakes here in Saskatchewan. The fly-in spots are world class— there's fresh air, fresh water and the shore lunches are to die for.

5. **Harvest Time on the Prairies**- There's a fresh smell in the air. It's like the whole province comes alive and everyone is filled with energy. Families and friends come together for hard work, which is the cornerstone of this province.

- 1995: Anne Szumigalski, *Voice*
- 1992: Maggie Siggins, *Revenge of the Land: A Century of Greed, Tragedy and Murder on a Saskatchewan Farm*
- 1989: Robert Calder, *Willie: The Life of W. Somerset Maugham*
- 1985: Frederick Wah, *Waiting for Saskatchewan*
- 1982: Guy Vanderhaeghe, *Man Descending: Selected Stories*
- Number of Governor General's Literary Award finalists from Saskatchewan: 20

GILLER PRIZE FINALISTS FROM SASKATCHEWAN:
- Sandra Birdsell, *The Russlander* (2001)
- Guy Vanderhaeghe, *The Englishman's Boy* (1996)

Source: Canada Council for the Arts.

Take 5 TOP FIVE MUSICIANS FROM SASKATCHEWAN

1. **Joni Mitchell:** Labeled the female Bob Dylan, Mitchell achieved fame in the late 1960s and was considered a key part of the Southern California folk rock scene.

2. **Colin James**, Canadian blues legend: James opened for Stevie Ray Vaughan in Regina. Vaughan was so impressed with James's performance that he invited him to open several tour dates. Vaughan gave James his stage name and James has since toured with Keith Richards of the Rolling Stones.

3. **Wide Mouth Mason:** Together since high school, the trio has two Certified Gold Records in Canada under their belt.

4. **Brad Johner:** A successful run with brother Ken as The Johner Brothers led to four hit albums before Johner was nominated for a Juno with his solo debut Free.

5. **The Northern Pikes:** Formed in Saskatoon in 1984, the Pikes found their biggest success with "She Ain't Pretty," which landed a Juno nomination.

Take 5 TOP FIVE MUSEUMS
BY ATTENDANCE

1. **MacKenzie Art Gallery,** Regina
2. **Western Development Museum,** Saskatoon
3. **Saskatchewan Science Centre,** Regina
4. **Royal Saskatchewan Museum,** Regina
5. **RCMP Heritage Centre,** Regina

Source: Museums Association of Saskatchewan.

DINING

- Number of bars, restaurants and caterers in the province: 1,725
- Number of people employed in restaurant industry: 31,800
- Industry sales annually: $1.3 billion
- Industry share of provincial GDP: 3.0 percent
- Foodservice share of provincial workforce: 6.5 percent

Source: Canadian Restaurant and Foodservices Association.

FAST FOOD

- Number of McDonald's in Canada: over 1,400
- Number of McDonald's in Saskatchewan: 37
- Number of Tim Horton's in Canada: 2,637
- Number of Tim Horton's in Saskatchewan: 34
- Number of Subways in Canada: 2,238
- Number of Subways in Saskatchewan: 70

Source: McDonald's; Tim Horton's; Subway.

BEER

- Brewpubs in Saskatchewan: 18
- Microbreweries in Saskatchewan: 1 (Great Western Brewing Company, Saskatoon)
- Brewery clubs and associations in Saskatchewan: 2

Take 5 — FIVE SASKATCHEWAN ACTORS

1. **Leslie Nielsen:** "The Naked Gun" and "Airplane!"
2. **Brent Butt:** "Corner Gas"
3. **Andrea Menard:** "Moccasin Flats" and "The Velvet Devil"
4. **Tom Jackson:** "North of 60"
5. **Arthur Hill:** "Who's Afraid of Virginia Woolf," "Andromeda Strain," "Owen Marshall" and "Counsellor at Law."

WINE

- Growers Wine Company, Moose Jaw, operated from 1964 to 1981
- Cypress Hills Vineyard and Winery opened on June 1, 2007

BUNNOCK: ANKLE BONE BASICS

Bunnock (meaning bones) originated in Russia and was brought to Canada by Russian Germans who settled at Macklin, SK (population 1,500). The game's 52 pieces are real horse ankle bones. Each team of four people has 26 bones. Twenty-two of the bones are lined up in a row on the ground in front of one team. The other team's 22 bones are lined up parallel to the first set 10 metres away. The object of the game is to knock over the other team's bunnocks by throwing yours one at a time, underhand from behind your line of bones. Points are awarded according to which bones and how many are hit. The first team to knock out all the other team's bones wins. It sounds easy but bone bowling/tossing takes skill.

Take 5 — FIVE SASKATCHEWAN-MADE MOVIES OR TV SHOWS

1. **"Corner Gas"**
2. **"Prairie Giant, The Tommy Douglas Story"**
3. **"Little Mosque on the Prairie"**
4. **"The Messengers"**
5. **"Renegade Press"**

Bio "MR. HOCKEY"

The career of Saskatchewan's greatest hockey export, Gordie Howe, began on Saskatoon's frozen ponds and sloughs. Born Gordon Howe in Floral, Saskatchewan on March 31, 1928, the man revered as "Mr. Hockey" overcame boyhood poverty to become an NHL legend. From his 1946 draft to the NHL at age 18, to his final retirement in 1980, Howe's career was full of records and accolades.

As a Detroit Red Wing, Howe led his team to four Stanley Cups and played on the famed "Production Line" with Ted Lindsay and Sid Abel. In 1963, he established a record for all time goals – a record that would last 36 years until it was broken by Wayne Gretzky.

At the end of the 1970-71 season, Howe retired. It was short-lived. In 1973-74, 45-year-old Howe came out of retirement to fulfill a lifelong dream of playing with his two sons, Mark and Marty, who played with the Houston Aeros of the World Hockey Association (WHA). For two years, Howe led the Aeros to the WHA championship, earning MVP honours on the way. When the WHA folded in 1979, the Hartford Whalers joined the NHL and the 51-year-old Howe returned to the NHL for all 80 games of his final season of 1979-80. That final year marked the sixth that he had played with his sons. It also saw another of Howe's dreams fulfilled as he and his sons played on the same NHL line.

By his retirement in 1980, Howe had amassed all-time records for goals, assists, points, games played, all star appearances, MVPs, scoring titles and seasons played. For 20 consecutive years he had been in the top five in NHL scoring. All the more remarkable was the fact that according to the stats, Howe had his best years at ages 41 and 48.

Howe was the first to win the Lester Patrick Trophy for outstanding service to hockey in the U.S, and is a member of 11 different Hall of Fames. He reached another milestone in 1997 when he signed a one-game contract with the Detroit Vipers of the International Hockey League. At nearly 70 years of age, Howe returned to the ice for one shift which allowed him to boast that he played professional hockey for an unprecedented six consecutive decades.

Macklin awards $30,000 in prize money during the two-day World Bunnock Championship held each August. Not surprisingly, people come from near and far to participate. Hosting 320 teams, Macklin's population doubles during the event which injects a half million dollars into the local economy. If you happen to be in Macklin, check out the 32-foot fiberglass, steel and mesh bone created by taxidermist Ray Berg of Cabri, Saskatchewan. Fittingly, the bunnock behemoth is the town's tourist information booth.

Did you know...

that famed theorist/physicist Albert Einstein played goal for the Canwood (Sk.) Canucks one winter while sojourning north to Canada to "find peace and silence" for his work on the Theory of Relativity? He had played hockey in his younger years in Germany.

Weblinks

Saskatchewan Arts Board

www.artsboard.sk.ca

This site provides information about current arts events in communities across Saskatchewan, arts awards and arts education programs and events.

Saskatchewan Craft Council

www.culturalindustries.sk.ca/crafts.shtml

A must-view for anyone interested in Saskatchewan crafts, this site lists Saskatchewan artisans who work in a variety of fields as well as the retail galleries that sell their wares. It also describes current exhibitions and crafts markets.

Saskatchewan Recording Industry Association

www.saskrecording.ca

This site offers an easy to navigate, categorized listing of all musicians who are members of the SRIA.

Saskatchewan Sports Hall of Fame

www.sshfm.com

Want to know the winningest teams in Saskatchewan's history? This site offers lists of all individuals and teams who have been inducted into the Saskatchewan Sports Hall of Fame since 1966.

Economy

Provincial real GDP forecast for 2012 has Saskatchewan taking over the lead (from Newfoundland and Labrador last year) with a solid rate of 4.6%, followed by Alberta (3.9%), and Manitoba (3.4%). It expected to be a big turnaround from 2009, when Saskatchewan's economy was hit by the global slowdown and declining commodity prices, and shrank by 3.0 per cent.

The truth is the Saskatchewan's economy has been out-performing the national average rate of GDP growth over the past three years, and has recently joined the small group of "have" provinces in Canada.

Growth is being fuelled by an expected strengthening in natural resource prices for potash, oil, natural gas and grains. Saskatchewan is also expected to have Canada's lowest unemployment rate in 2012 (4.8 per cent) and 2013 (4.6 per cent).

Provincial finances are also now in much better shape. The province received 13 consecutive credit rating upgrades. One of Saskatchewan's biggest challenges will be to deal with serious labour shortages for several sectors in the province.

GROSS DOMESTIC PRODUCT

- In 2010, Saskatchewan's real Gross Domestic Product (GDP) totaled $41.5 billion, an increase of 4.0% from 2009. Saskatchewan's real growth rate was second among the provinces in 2010.

TOP FIVE EXPENSES OF SASKATCHEWAN HOUSEHOLDS

1. **Income tax** ($10,792 or 18.7 percent)
2. **Shelter** ($9,924 or 17.2 percent)
3. **Transportation** ($8,387 or 14.5 percent)
4. **Food** ($5,854 or 10.1 percent)
5. **Recreation** ($3,742 or 6.5 percent)

Source: Statistics Canada.

- Per capita GDP in 2010 stood at $41,024
- Saskatchewan's in 2011: 4.3 percent
- National GDP growth for the same period: 3.1 percent

Source: Statistics Canada.

TAXES

- Provincial sales tax: 5 percent
- Personal income tax rates: 11 percent to 15 percent
- Small business corporate tax rate: 4.5 percent
- Large business corporate tax rate: 13 percent (12 percent as of July 1, 2008)

TAX FREEDOM DAY

Tax freedom day (day on which earnings no longer go to taxes (2011) is June 6 nationally).

- Alberta: May 18
- New Brunswick: May 31

They Said It

"Don't let anybody delude you into thinking it's not a competitive environment."

– Brandt Randles, President, Louis Dreyfus Canada, Yorkton This Week, October 18, 2006, commenting on Saskatchewan's economy.

- Ontario: June 1
- Prince Edward Island: May 27
- Manitoba: June 1
- British Columbia: June 6
- Nova Scotia: June 7
- Quebec June 10
- Newfoundland and Labrador: June 19
- **Saskatchewan: June 6**

Source: The Fraser Institute.

Take 5 PAUL MARTIN'S TOP FIVE FAVOURITE THINGS ABOUT DOING BUSINESS IN SASKATCHEWAN

Paul Martin is a writer, broadcaster and entrepreneur who has chronicled the activities of Saskatchewan's commercial community for three decades as a business editor of a daily newspaper, host of a television show and commentator on more than a dozen Saskatchewan radio stations. Along with operating his own businesses, he chairs the board of the Regina Regional Economic Development Authority.

1. There's room to grow and lots of it.

2. The Canadian Light Source Synchrotron, Canada's largest scientific investment in a half century.

3. We're Canada's next breakthrough region; if you subscribe to the theory of Buy Low, Sell High, get in now because we're poised to take off!

4. We have a diversified resource base including oil, gas and tar sands as well as the world's biggest supplies of uranium and potash.

5. Our endless horizons; it's so flat you can see the future from here!

Take 5 SASKATCHEWAN'S LARGEST EMPLOYERS (BY NUMBER OF EMPLOYEES)

1. **Saskatoon Health Region** (11,250)
2. **Regina Qu'Appelle Health Region** (9,200)
3. **SaskTel** (3,321)
4. **SaskPower** (2,397)
5. **SIAST** (1,517)

Source: Saskatchewan Business Magazine

INFLATION

- In 2012, the inflation rate stood at 2.8 percent, up from 2.1 percent in 2006.

INCOME (2009)

Median family income in Saskatchewan: $65,120 (Canada: $66,550)
Real personal disposable income per capita in Saskatchewan: $21,953 (Canada: $24,099)

In 2009, Saskatchewan's workers earned an average $802.55 a week, just below the Canadian average of $822.42. Canada's highest wages were earned in the Northwest Territories ($1,149.64) and the lowest in Prince Edward Island ($690.01).

Sources: Institute of Chartered Accountants of Saskatchewan; Statistics Canada.

BUYING A HOUSE

As of January, 2010, the average house price in Saskatchewan was $228,000, up from $166,016 in 2007. Regionally, prices vary. Houses in Regina average $214,000 (up from $162,532 in 2007) and homes in Saskatoon average $335,251 (up from $233,917 in 2007). Homes in British Columbia average $492,000 (the highest) and homes in New Brunswick average $156,000 (the lowest). Nationally, the average price is $329,000.

Source: Canadian Real Estate Association.

Bio THE HILLS ARE ALIVE

Soon after Saskatchewan joined Confederation, school teacher Walter Hill and his partner E.A. McCallum started what would become one of the province's most enduring companies when the doors to their insurance and real estate business opened in Regina. The industrious duo developed housing areas throughout the city, the best known being the now historic Lakeview subdivision in the south end.

By 1912, McCallum-Hill was western Canada's largest land developer. When McCallum died in the 1930s, it became a Hill family enterprise. By 1953, Walter decided to enjoy the fruits of his labour and turned the family business over to his son Frederick W. Hill.

Although Frederick was just 33, he was already a veteran of the US air force and he quickly proved he was the man to head McCallum- Hill. He furthered the tradition of residential development with Hillsdale, Regina's first private subdivision. He also developed Regina's city centre, adding five new office towers downtown. Frederick's business acumen and his contributions to Regina's society and economy has earned him accolades. Frederick received the Order of Canada in 1986 and the Saskatchewan Order of Merit in 1999.

Today the Hill family business – which celebrated its 100th anniversary in 2003 – is Canada's oldest family-run real estate company. It is now run by Paul Hill, a third generation Hill. The company remains heavily involved in real estate; it owns and manages more than 1.85 million square feet in Saskatchewan and over 700,000 square feet in Alberta, as well as residential and commercial properties in Arizona and Texas. Today the Hills are also involved in broadcasting, insurance, oil and gas and manufacturing.

You Said How Much?

Select hourly wages in Saskatchewan

Judge	84.71
Petroleum engineer	40.39
Psychologist	36.51
Pharmacist	34.74
Geologists, geochemists, geophysicists	34.23
Editor	32.74
Bankers, credit and investment manager	32.30
Dental hygienist	32.30
Secondary school teacher	30.94
Fire chiefs/ senior officers	30.37
Petroleum, gas and chemical processor	29.86
Registered nurse	29.16
Computer programmer	28.53
Veterinarian	26.27
Electrical power line/cable worker	24.15
Ambulance attendants	21.40
Plumber	20.08
Sheet metal worker	19.31
Carpenter	19.28
Heavy equipment operator	17.86
Secretary	16.97
Truck driver	16.57
Store keeper	16.50
Butcher	15.87
Chef	15.01
Janitors/caretakers/building superintendents	13.16
Farm worker	12.25
Hairstylist/barber	12.23
Delivery driver	12.08
Early childhood educator	11.21
Cook	9.80
Taxi/ limo driver	9.42
Bartender	9.36
Cashier	8.59
Service station attendant	7.20

Source: Human Resources Canada

Take 5 SASKATCHEWAN'S HIGH SALARIES

1. **Scott Hartnell, NHL player originally from Regina:** $1,750,000
2. **Wayne Brownlee, CFO Potash Corp of Saskatchewan:** $13,900,000
3. **Kerry Joseph, Saskatchewan Roughrider Quarterback:** $225,000
4. **CEOs of SaskTel and SaskPower (minimum base salary):** $207,720
5. **Saskatchewan MLAs:** $73,173

Source: Saskatchewan Business Magazine

HOUSING COSTS

People of Saskatchewan shell out an average of $12,803 for shelter and household operation expenses. This represents about 22 percent of their total expenditures. Nationally, Canadians spend $15,705 for shelter and household operations – about 23.5 percent of their costs.

HOUSEHOLD EXPENDITURES

- Amount spent by Saskatchewan households: $57,734
- National household expenditure: $66,857
- Northwest Territories (the highest): $89,729
- Newfoundland and Labrador (the lowest): $52,612

Source: Statistics Canada.

EMPLOYMENT

Labour force	509,000
Employed	484,000
Unemployed	26,000
Unemployment Rate	5.1 percent
Participation Rate	68.1 percent

Take 5 SASKATCHEWAN'S TOP FIVE EXPORT INDUSTRIES (2006)

1. **Oil and gas extraction** (37.4 percent)
2. **Other non-metallic mineral mining and quarrying** (14.6 percent)
3. **Wheat farming** (11.3 percent)
4. **Oilseed** (except soybean) **farming** (5.4 percent)
5. **Dry pea and bean farming** (4.7 percent)

Source: Saskatchewan Industry and Resources.

BY THE HOUR

In 2010, workers in Saskatchewan earned an average hourly salary of $22.29

- Aged 15 to 24: $14.28
- Aged 25 to 54: $24.35
- Aged 55 and older: $23.48
- Men: $24.13
- Women: $20.48
- Part time: $15.78
- Full time: $23.82
- Unionized: $25.75
- Non-unionized: $20.40

Source: Statistics Canada.

HOW WE GET TO WORK

- Percentage who drive their own car or truck: 79.7
- Walk: 8.3
- Carpool: 6.7
- Public transit: 2.4

They Said It

"There is a reason the province is racking up record land sales: it's a great place to do business."

– Oilweek Magazine, April 2007

- Bicycle: 1.6
- Other: 1.1
- Taxi: 0.17
- Motorcycle: 0.12

Source: Statistics Canada.

A Grain of Truth

Agriculture remains a key economic sector, and wheat is still the cream of the crop. Saskatchewan wheat traces its roots to the Carrot River Valley in 1756. It took some time, but with the arrival of the CPR in the 1880s (which brought both farmers and a means of transporting the crop to market) and until the Great Depression of the 1930s, wheat was the province's main commercial crop. By the end of World War One, the lucrative crop covered four million hectares.

Even more significant to the wheat boom than the railway was the development of Marquis wheat by Charles Saunders in the early 1900s. Marquis matured early and produced larger yields and high quality flour. It was well-suited to Saskatchewan's northern growing season and soon came to dominate the province's fields. By the early 1920s more than 90 percent of western Canadian-grown spring wheat was of the Marquis variety.

Marquis wheat is the cornerstone of Canada's Western Red Spring wheat class, which today accounts for 85 percent of the province's common spring wheat. Other spring varieties include Canada Prairie Spring Red, Canada Prairie Spring White, Canada Western Extra Spring and Canada Western Soft White. Together these spring classes represent nearly 99 percent of all common wheat grown in the province. Only Canada Western Red Winter has a winter growth habit.

Durum wheat is the second most important Canadian wheat, and it has thrived in Saskatchewan since the 1920s. Today, Saskatchewan's durum is responsible for 83 percent of the total grown in the country.

Saskatchewan wheat adds $1.3 billion to the Saskatchewan economy annually.

Take 5 TOP FIVE GDP GENERATING INDUSTRIES (PERCENTAGE)

1. **Mining/Oil & Gas Extraction** (18.2 percent)
2. **Finance, Insurance, Real Estate and Rental & Leasing** (15 percent)
3. **Agriculture, Forestry, Fishing and Hunting** (8.2 percent)
4. **Manufacturing** (6.9 percent)
5. **Transportation and Warehousing** (6.3 percent)

Source: Government of Saskatchewan

TRANSPORTATION INFRASTRUCTURE

- Number of airports: 2 major (Saskatoon and Regina); 18 smaller
- Length of highways: 26,250 km
- Paved highway: 13,460 km
- Gravel highway: 5,700 km
- Ice highway: 131 km
- Trans-Canada Highway: 654 km
- Rail lines: 13,041

Sources: Government of Saskatchewan; TransCanada Highway Online; Encyclopedia of Saskatchewan (On-line).

EMPLOYMENT SECTORS

- Percentage who work in services: 21.0
- Percentage who work in education and healthcare: 19.9
- Percentage who work in trade: 16.1
- Percentage who work in agriculture: 9.7
- Percentage who work in construction: 6.0
- Percentage who work in manufacturing: 6.0
- Percentage who work in public administration: 5.6
- Percentage who work in transportation, warehousing and other utilities: 5.2

- Percentage who work in finance, insurance, real estate and leasing: 5.2
- Percentage who work in other primary industries: 4.4
- Percentage who work in utilities: 0.9

PUBLIC ADMINISTRATION AND BEYOND

- One in every 36 people in the province – or one in 18 employed people – works for the government or for a government agency.
- Percentage who work for local, municipal, regional and aboriginal governments: 29.8
- Percentage who work for the provincial government: 37.8
- Percentage who work for the federal government (including defense services): 32.4
- The people who work in Public Administration are part of the 113,700 people who work in the public sector, which also includes education and health sectors. Another 263,500 people work in the private sector, while just fewer than 99,000 people in Saskatchewan are self-employed.

Source: Saskatchewan Industry and Resources.

CREDIT UNIONS

Credit unions have long been important in the financial lives of Saskatchewanians.

- Number of credit unions: 64
- Number of communities served: 283
- Credit union assets: $10.1 billion
- Revenue: $675 million
- Amount lent to members: $7.7 billion
- Amount returned to members: $22 million
- People employed by credit unions: 3,300

Source: Saskatchewan Credit Unions.

Take 5 SASKATCHEWAN'S TOP FIVE IMPORT INDUSTRIES (2006)

1. **Construction machinery manufacturing** (12 percent)
2. **Motor vehicle body and trailer manufacturing** (5.9 percent)
3. **Agricultural implement manufacturing** (5.3 percent)
4. **Heavy duty truck manufacturing** (5.3 percent)
5. **Engine, turbine and power transmission equipment manufacturing** (4.6 percent)

Source: Saskatchewan Industry and Resources.

BUSINESS

- Percentage of businesses that employ fewer than five people: 7
- Percentage with 5-19 employees: 15
- Percentage with 20-49 employees: 10
- Percentage with 50-299 employees: 16
- Percentage with 300-499 employees: 4
- Percentage with 500 employees or more: 48

SMALL BUSINESSES

- Saskatchewan is home to 39,000 small businesses which account for 95 percent of the province's business.
- Number who work for small businesses: 140,000 (36 percent of the workforce)
- Amount generated by small business annually: $3.34 billion
- Percentage of small businesses that are rural: 42

Sources: Government of Saskatchewan; New Democratic Party - NDP Caucus - Saskatchewan; Government of Canada.

EXPORTS

- Total value of Saskatchewan's exports: $30 billion
- Exports as percentage of GDP (income based): 35 percent
- Exports as percentage of national GDP: 1.1 percent

Source: Statistics Canada.

AGRICULTURE

While the province has spent the better part of the last decade diversifying its economy, agriculture is still a key sector. Agriculture and its related industries were responsible for over 31 percent of the province's 2006 exports. Despite the fact that the number of farms and total farm area are declining, farm production and total cash receipts are on the rise. Since 1986, the number of farms in Saskatchewan has decreased by about 30 percent to just over 44,000 in 2006. Though the total number of farms and the area they cover is getting smaller, individual farms themselves are not. In the 20 years between 1986 and 2006, farms in the province increased in size from an average 419 hectares to 587 hectares. Total cash receipts for 2008 were at $9.5 billion, up from $6.6 billion in 2006.

Everyone in the pool

One of the province's most successful co-operatives and corporations is the Saskatchewan Wheat Pool (SWP). Formed in 1923 as the Saskatchewan Co-operative Wheat Producers and renamed in 1953, the pool was a central marketing organization for grain producers. Farmers throughout the prairies pooled their revenues and divided them so every contributor would receive the same price for each grade of grain. The pools owned and controlled their own selling agency, which helped them deal directly with overseas markets and compete with other grain consortiums. The Great Depression nearly bankrupted the pool and forced it to abandon marketing and focus as an elevator co-operative. It had great success; between the early 1970s and 1992, the SWP handled more than 60 percent of the province's grain and generated $73 million in earnings. Millions in losses followed, however, forcing the organization into debt restructuring, facility cutbacks and the unusual step for a co-op of listing publicly. The changes have nevertheless had a positive impact. Today, the pool employs more than 2,500 people, manages a wage bill of over $100 million and, in 2004, posted its first net profit in six years.

FARM DEBT

Saskatchewan farm debt stands at $7.02 billion, the fourth highest in the country. The share of debt held by chartered banks was 29 percent, while federal agencies accounted for 31 percent and credit unions 25 percent.

IF A TREE FALLS ON THE PRAIRIE

It may be something of a surprise to realize that more than half of Saskatchewan is forested. Over 90 percent of its forests grow on Crown land, with nine provincial forests covering over 35 million hectares or nearly 55 percent of the province. Saskatchewan's forest sector contributes over $1 billion a year to the provincial economy. There are more than 300 firms employing as many as 5,000 people during normal market periods. Saskatchewan also has more than 100 firms involved in secondary wood products manufacturing.

Saskatchewan's forest industry has four primary sectors: softwood lumber, pulp, plywood and engineered wood products.

OIL AND GAS

In 2006, more than 38 percent of Saskatchewan's export value came from oil and gas, the province's most important sector. Saskatchewan produces 20 percent of Canada's oil and gas, making it the second most important oil and gas producing province after Alberta.

Commercial crude was first discovered in 1944. By 2006, more than 7,100 wells had been drilled — 2,339 in 2006, the second highest number on record. Saskatchewan's first commercial natural gas well was drilled in 1934. By the end of 2006 there were nearly 18,700 and Saskatchewan was third in Canada in natural gas production.

Did you know...

that 44 percent of all the cultivated farmland in Canada is in Saskatchewan?

Saskatchewan's oil and gas industry provided almost $1.7 billion in revenue to the province in 2007-08. The industry is also one of the largest contributors to the provincial economy at nine per cent of the GDP.

OIL AND GAS FACTS

Saskatchewan accounts for 28 per cent of the country's primary energy production, the highest of all provinces in Canada.

- Saskatchewan is Canada's second largest oil producer, and the fifth largest oil producer among all American states and Canadian provinces. Our conventional oil in place is estimated at 45.6 billion barrels.
- The province is home to a significant portion of one of the hottest oil plays in North America — the Bakken Formation.
- Oil production was 154 million barrels in 2010; value of sales was approximately $10.8 billion.
- Revenue to the province from the sale of Crown petroleum and natural gas rights was $463 million in 2010.
- Saskatchewan is the third largest producer of natural gas and coal in Canada.

Source: Government of Saskatchewan.

Farm Country

Saskatchewan supplies more than 10 per cent of the world's total exported wheat. More than 70 grain, oilseeds, pulses and special crops are grown in Saskatchewan. The province is the leading Canadian producer of wheat, canola, durum, flax, oats, barley, dry peas, lentils, chickpeas, oats, forage and grass seed, rye, canary seed, wild rice and organic grain. Quite naturally then, the province has developed strong milling and oil-crushing sectors. Saskatchewan is home to almost 30 per cent of Canada's beef herd and about 10 per cent of the Canadian hog inventory. The province has the second-largest bison herd in the country.

Take 5 TOP FIVE CROPS GROWN IN SASKATCHEWAN (BY VALUE)

1. **Wheat - including durum** ($1.34 billion)
2. **Canola** ($1.11 billion)
3. **Dry peas** ($2.47 million)
4. **Lentils** ($2.06 million)
5. **Oats** ($1.75 million)

Source: Saskatchewan Industry and Resources.

MINING AND METALS

Mining is Saskatchewan's third largest industry sector after oil and gas and agriculture. The province is a mineral powerhouse and the sector employs more than 24,000 people directly and indirectly and contributes more than $3 billion annually to the economy in wages, goods and services, taxes and fees. Exploration expenditures are expected to top $290 million for 2009. According to Natural Resources Canada, Saskatchewan accounted for 16 per cent of Canada's exploration expenditures in 2009, third highest in the country.

MINERAL FACTS

- Saskatchewan is one of the world's leading uranium producers, accounting for approximately 20 per cent of global production.
- Uranium deposits are the richest in the world and are the equivalent of 19 billion barrels of oil or four billion tonnes of coal.
- Saskatchewan is the world's largest producer of potash, a mineral critical to the fertilizer that global crops need. The mines account for roughly 30 per cent of world potash production, and potash companies have announced almost $13 billion worth of expansions to their existing mines by 2020.
- Saskatchewan's value of mineral production was over $6.8 billion in 2010, with mineral exploration expenditures at $319 million. Mineral exploration spending intentions in 2011 are estimated at approximately $280 million.

They Said It

"*The Lord said 'let there be wheat' and Saskatchewan was born.*"

– Author and humourist Stephen Leacock

BURNING THE MIDNIGHT (CANOLA) OIL

Numerous companies in the province are on the cutting edge. One of these is Milligan Bio-Tech. The company is a value added one in that it is looking for ways to create environmentally responsible products from off grade and heated Canola oil. After years of hard work and testing, teaming with industry partners and members of the scientific community, the company's work is catching on. Since beginning production of its bio-fuels line in 2001, Milligan Bio-Tech has nearly doubled its sales every year, and has continuously expanded to meet growing demands. The company opened a crushing plant to generate oil for bio-diesel products in 2006, and its current product line includes bio-diesel, diesel fuel conditioner, penetrating oil and a road dust suppressant.

Did you know...

that Saskatchewan's highway and municipal road networks together constitute the largest rural road system in Canada, totaling over 190,000 km?

Take 5 TOP FIVE DESTINATIONS OF SASKATCHEWAN EXPORTS

1. **United States** (66.7 percent)
2. **China** (3.1 percent)
3. **Japan** (3.1 percent)
4. **United Kingdom** (2.9 percent)
5. **India** (2.4 percent)

Source: Saskatchewan Industry and Resources.

WHEN PIGS FLY

It was two centuries ago that the Mendel family in Westphalia, Germany slaughtered their first pig and opened what would become a thriving meat packing business. Within a generation, Robert Mendel started packing and selling canned hams around the continent. By 1940 Europe's turmoil was too much for Robert's son Fred. He packed his suitcase, some canned hams, and turned an eye toward Saskatoon.

He quickly started a new company called Intercontinental Packers. Within 10 years the company was expanding, purchasing along the way Prairie Packers in Regina, and later a plant in Vancouver. By 1970 it was time for Fred to hand over control of the ship to his daughter, Johanna Mitchell, who had been director of the company since its doors opened. Six years later her son Fred – a fifth generation meat man – took over, launching the Mitchell Gourmet Foods line the company is so well known for today.

Did you know...

that downtown Regina is home to Canada's largest free wireless internet zone? With a start up cost of $1.3 million, the wireless network will cost an estimated $340,000 a year to maintain. Business districts in three other Saskatchewan cities – Regina, Moose Jaw, Saskatoon and Prince Alberta – can also log on to the system.

Take 5 TOP FIVE ORIGINS OF SASKATCHEWAN IMPORTS

1. **United States** (88.1 percent)
2. **China** (2.0 percent)
3. **Germany** (1.7 percent)
4. **Mexico** (1.2 percent)
5. **France** (0.9 percent)

Source: Saskatchewan Industry and Resources.

Since then, the company has partnered with and then was bought out by the Schneider Corporation. Mitchell Gourmet Foods remains an independent operating company of Schneider Foods, following in the footsteps of quality and tradition first taken in Saskatchewan by Fred Mandel more than 65 years ago.

POTASH

Saskatchewan's rich potash deposits were discovered by accident in the 1940s through petroleum exploration drilling. Saskatchewan potash is found in the Prairie Formation, which lies at depths greater than 1000 m beneath much of southern Saskatchewan. The potash reserves in Saskatchewan are massive. By conservative estimates, Saskatchewan could supply world demand at current levels for several hundred years.

Potash production in Saskatchewan has been continuous since 1962, when IMC Global opened the K-1 mine at Esterhazy. By 1971,

They Said It

"Let me remind you that we believe in a mixed economy of public ownership, co-operative ownership, and private ownership. The problem was deciding which businesses belong to each category. There were some things we did, not because they belonged in the public ownership category, but because there was no one else to do them."

— **Tommy Douglas speaking on the CCF economic ideology.**

the 10 potash mines currently operating were all in production. The industry's capital investment is over $2.5 billion.

The province is the largest potash producer in the world and accounts for about one third of world potash production. In recent years, annual sales for Saskatchewan potash has totalled some $1 billion per year.

Saskatchewan's competitive advantage is the exceptional extent and quality of its ore reserves. The high-grade ore lies in basically flat beds, allowing the use of highly efficient mining techniques.

Only about five per cent of the potash produced in Saskatchewan is consumed in Canada. About two-thirds of the exports go to the U.S., where Saskatchewan potash fills approximately 70 per cent of the market demand. The province is also a major supplier to the large Pacific Rim offshore markets: China, Japan, Malaysia, Korea and Indonesia. All Saskatchewan producers make offshore sales through Canpotex, a Saskatoon-based marketing company owned by its member companies.

URANIUM

The discovery and development of uranium deposits in Saskatchewan happened in the Beaverlodge District, on the north shore of Lake Athabasca. Prospectors searching for gold and copper were the first to notice uranium mineralization in the early 1930s.

When uranium's economic importance became recognized, extensive prospecting eventually led to the establishment of the Uranium City mining camp. In the 1950s, 16 ore bodies and three separate milling facilities were developed in the Uranium City area. Saskatchewan is currently the largest uranium-producing region in the world and accounts for about 30 per cent of annual world uranium production.

The richest uranium deposits in the world occur at or near the base of the Athabasca Basin sandstone sequence. Uranium ore in Saskatchewan is mined by both underground and open pit mining methods. Uranium deposits in Saskatchewan's contain high-grade ore and can be extracted at production costs below those in many other parts of the world. Saskatchewan's uranium resources are sufficient for more than 40 years at current rates of production.

There are currently three uranium mining operations in the province; Eagle Point, McArthur River and McClean Lake. Uranium is sold by the mining companies to electric power utilities in Canada, the United States, Europe and the Far East. Saskatchewan's uranium mining industry is expected to remain competitive well into the future due to its substantial, lower-cost, high-grade uranium resources.

Weblinks

Saskatchewan Wheat Pool

www.swp.com

Canada's largest publicly traded agri-business co-operative, with operations in grain handling and marketing, farm supplies, agri-food processing and much more.

Saskjobs.ca

www.saskjobs.ca

Need a job? Look here, where you can search by area, post your resume online and follow quick links to 7 other Saskatchewan job ad websites.

Saskatchewan Credit Unions

www.saskcu.com

General information about Saskatchewan credit unions with links to help you locate your closest credit union.

Politics

Much of Saskatchewan's political development has been the response to the settlement experience. It has been proudly independent and self sufficient on the one hand, yet recognizing the power and importance of collective solutions on the other. Like many other parts of Canada with large landscape and few people, solutions often defy easy political categories.

Saskatchewan was home to Canada's self-proclaimed socialist government in 1944. It was also the first province to introduce government funded mandatory universal medical insurance. Much of the post war years have been dominated by the left leaning CCF and its successor the New Democratic Party. Apart from a Liberal blip in the 1960s and a Conservative blip in the 1980s, Saskatchewan continued to be dominated by the New Democratic Party until 2007, when the Saskatchewan Party was voted to the top.

GOVERNANCE BEFORE GOVERNMENT

The arrival of Europeans came with the Hudson's Bay Company (HBC). In the mid-17th century, two men – Chouard Des Groseillers and Pierre-Esprit Radisson – dreamed of a North American trading company. When their pitch to the French government was rejected, the undaunted duo turned to the British who, in 1670, granted the men a Royal charter giving them a trade monopoly over the vast Rupert's land.

The HBC established the first vestiges of European political order as a series of HBC forts sprung up across the west and an HBC bureaucracy emerged. Headed by a Governor, the HBC was authorized to establish rules and regulations in the western North American region that is Saskatchewan, Manitoba, Alberta, Ontario, Quebec, the Yukon and the Northwest Territories.

In 1870, the three-year old country of Canada purchased Rupert's Land and the Northwestern Territory from the HBC, renaming them both the Northwest Territories.

OTTAWA TAKES OVER

When Canada assumed control of the new Northwest Territories, the federal government passed the "Act for the temporary government of Rupert's Land and the Northwestern Territory when united with Canada," giving decision-making power to a local interim government consisting of Lieutenant-Governor and a council appointed by Ottawa. The first Lieutenant-Governor, William McDougall, had authority over such matters as road construction and maintenance, inheritance, public health and alcohol control.

In 1875, Canada passed the "Northwest Territories Act" and appointed David Laird the Lieutenant-Governor. Unlike the interim government, Laird's council was elected and the Act stipulated that the number of elected council representatives would grow with the territory's population. In March of 1877 the elected council held its first meeting. In 1886 the territory got an official legislative assembly and a year later Ottawa granted the Northwest Territories four seats in the House of Commons.

GOVERNMENT DOUGH: WHERE SASKATCHEWAN GETS ITS CASH

Total revenue	$12.1 billion
Percentage from income taxes	19.5 percent
Consumption taxes	17.5 percent
Property and related taxes	15.2 percent
Investment income	14.8 percent
Sales of goods and services	11.8 percent
Specific purpose transfers	11.0 percent
Other taxes	5.3 percent
General purpose transfers	2.8 percent
Contributions to social security plans	2.1 percent

SPENDING THE DOUGH: WHERE SASKATCHEWAN SPENDS ITS CASH

Total expenditures	$11.99 billion
Health	27.9 percent
Education	23.3 percent
Social services	9.5 percent
Transportation and communication	7.7 percent
Debt charges	6.7 percent
Resource conservation/industrial development	6.5 percent
Protection of persons and property	6.0 percent
Environment	3.0 percent
Percentage on general government services	2.9 percent
Recreation and culture	2.8 percent
Housing	2.1 percent
Surplus	0.83 percent
Other expenditures	0.74 percent
Regional planning and development	0.42 percent
General purpose transfers	0.13 percent
Labour, employment and immigration	0.13 percent
Research establishments	0.07 percent

SASKATCHEWAN IS BORN

In 1897, the Northwest Territories was granted responsible government. Still, territorial officials were not pleased with their position in Canada. A federal immigration campaign introduced in 1896 had succeeded in boosting the Territories' population. The problem was that while the Territories had provincial-style responsibilities, it did not have provincial-style funding. The new schools, public works, and demands for services that came with the larger population strained the limited Territorial bank account.

Bio TOMMY DOUGLAS:
THE FATHER MEDICARE AND
SON OF SASKATCHEWAN

Douglas was born in 1904 in Falkirk, Scotland. When he was ten years old, a leg infection threatened to take his leg. Although they were not poor, the services of a specialist were beyond the Douglas family's means. It was only thanks to an orthopedic surgeon who believed young Douglas' case would make a good teaching opportunity for his medical students that Douglas underwent surgery to save the limb. This experience fostered in Douglas a life-long commitment to the ideal of free universal healthcare.

In 1910, the Douglas family moved to Winnipeg. It was there he attended university and by 1930 was an ordained minister in the Baptist church. Joined by his wife, Irma, Douglas assumed his first charge in Weyburn and earned a reputation as a fine orator. Douglas' first years in ministry, which coincided with the Great Depression, were difficult and he devoted himself to helping the needy. But for Douglas this was not enough and he took his desire to improve society from the pulpit into politics.

In 1932, Douglas became president of the Weyburn Independent Labour Party, a party which, in 1934, merged with the CCF. In 1935, CCFer Douglas won a seat in the federal House of Commons. His first federal career was cut short when, in 1942, he

Sir Frederick William Gordon Haultain, the Territories' de facto premier, proposed that the Territory become self-governing. Prime Minister Wilfrid Laurier met with Haultain and other territorial officials to discuss the matter. A bill proposing the unification of the districts of Assiniboia, Saskatchewan, Alberta and Athabasca as a single province, with the same powers and responsibilities possessed by the other provinces, was presented to the premier. Haultain recommended the province control its own Crown lands, that that it receive $50,000 plus a per capita grant of 80

was elected leader of the provincial CCF. Two years later, Douglas led the CCF to a landslide victory.

As premier, Douglas introduced state-controlled travel, communication and insurance. He addressed worker rights and improved the conditions under which they laboured. The pinnacle of his achievement came only after he had left provincial politics to lead the federal NDP. In 1961, months after leaving provincial politics, Douglas' years of lobbying paid off when Medicare was implemented in Saskatchewan.

Douglas led the NDP in the House of Commons for a decade. Although he never became Prime Minister, Douglas' ideas were influential across the nation. In 1967, Liberal Prime Minister Lester B. Pearson, having faced much pressure from Douglas, introduced Canada's first national Medicare system. By 1972, all provinces and territories had accepted the plan.

Cancer claimed Douglas in 1986. Since then, his persona has been elevated to the status of "Prairie Giant," as one CBC miniseries called him. In 2004, the CBC orchestrated a national contest to name the Greatest Canadian. Douglas won, beating out such Canadians as Sir John A. Macdonald, Terry Fox and Wayne Gretzky.

cents per person up to $200,000. Then talks stalled for several years.

In 1904, Haultain requested the resumption of negotiations. Prime Minister Laurier replied that although he was preoccupied with an election bid, he would, if re-elected, resolve the Northwest Territories provincial question. Laurier won and kept his promise.

In January 1905, talks resumed. Haultain conceded that given the vast size of the region, the territory should be divided into two separate provinces, Saskatchewan and Alberta. He insisted that the new provinces control their Crown lands. Laurier refused, arguing that Ottawa needed to retain Crown land in order to fulfill plans for western settlement. Despite this point of disagreement, negotiations succeeded. On September 1, 1905, Saskatchewan and Alberta officially became Canadian provinces. Ottawa retained control of Crown lands until 1930.

SASKATCHEWAN PREMIERS AND THEIR OCCUPATIONS

Premier	Party	Term	Occupation
Walter Scott	Lib	1905-1916	newspaper editor
William Martin	Lib	1916-1922	teacher, lawyer
Charles Dunning	Lib	1922-1926	iron worker, farmhand
James Gardiner	Lib	1926-1929; 1934-1935	farmer
James Anderson	Cons	1929-1934	school inspector
William Patterson	Lib	1935-1944	banker, lawyer
Tommy Douglas	CCF	1944-1961	Baptist minister
Woodrow Lloyd	CCF	1961-1964	teacher
Ross Thatcher	Lib	1964-1971	city alderman
Allan Blakeney	NDP	1971-1982	civil servant
Grant Devine	Cons	1982-1991	economist, professor
Roy Romanow	NDP	1991-2001	lawyer
Lorne Calvert	NDP	2001-2007	United Church minister
Brad Wall	SK	2007-	businessman

Women in Politics

1912: The Saskatchewan Grain Growers Association passes a resolution calling for women's suffrage.

1915: 11,000 women sign a petition demanding the franchise. It is disregarded.

1916: Saskatchewan women earn the right to vote and to hold office provincially.

1919: Liberal Sarah Ramsland becomes the first female MLA in Saskatchewan.

1940: Dorise Nielsen, UP, becomes the first female MP from Saskatchewan.

1945: Florence McOrmond is elected mayor of Sutherland in 1945; she is the first female mayor in the province.

1956: For the first time, two women are elected in the same provincial election: Marjorie Cooper, UP and Mary Jane Batten, Liberal.

1982: Progressive Conservatives Joan Duncan and Patricia Smith the first women appointed to the Saskatchewan cabinet.

1982: The first woman Cabinet Minister, Joan Heather Duncan, is made Minister of Government Services.

1984: Jeanne Sauvé, born in Prud'homme, is the first woman to be named Governor General.

1988: Sylvia O. Fedoruk is the first female Lieutenant-Governor of Saskatchewan.

1989: Lynda Haverstock, Liberal, is the first female leader of a Saskatchewan political party.

1993: Raynell Andreychuk, becomes the first woman to represent Saskatchewan in Canada's Senate.

2003: Joan Beatty, NDP, is the first Aboriginal woman elected MLA.

POLITICAL TRENDS

Liberal red coloured Saskatchewan's political map from 1905 to 1929. Lead by James T.M. Anderson, the Conservatives took office briefly in 1929, only to have power snapped back by the Liberals five years later.

Liberals remained in control until Tommy Douglas' Co-operative Commonwealth Federation (CCF) began a two decade stint in 1944. In 1964, the Liberals of Ross Thatcher began seven years of rule. Then, in 1971, Allan Blakeney brought back the left with his New Democratic Party. In 1982 Grant Devine's Conservatives assumed office.

Nine years passed before the NDP again formed a government. In 1991, Roy Romanow reclaimed the province for the NDP. In 2001, Lorne Calvert assumed the leadership of the NDP and was elected premier. He was re-elected in 2003. It remained in NDP hands until the 2007 election, when Brad Wall and his Saskatchewan Party were voted in.

JOURNEY FROM TRAGEDY TO TRIUMPH

With the death of her husband in November 1918, Sarah Katherine Ramsland suffered one of the greatest losses of her life. Less than a year later, she experienced one of her greatest victories.

Running in the July 1919 by-election to fill the seat vacated by her late

Did you know...

that only five percent of Saskatchewan's MLAs have been female?

husband, she became the first woman elected to the Legislative Assembly of Saskatchewan as a member of the Liberal Party for the Pelly constituency. Saskatchewan women had only won the right to vote three years earlier.

The highlight of her political career was her introduction of a resolution calling for amendments to the divorce laws that would allow men and women to apply on equal grounds. This milestone motion received the unanimous support of the members of the Assembly.

The Saskatchewan Party

The Saskatchewan Party was born in 1997 as the Saskatchewan Liberals struggled with internal division and the Conservatives were reeling from fraud scandals. As the future looked bleak for both parties, four Conservative and four Liberal MLAs merged to form the right-wing Saskatchewan Party.

The new party quickly surpassed the Liberal Party in the Legislature to become the official opposition. Reflecting its right-leaning orientation, the first party leader was former Reform Party MP, Elwin Hermanson. He was elected to this post in April 1998.

Controversy quickly surrounded the Saskatchewan Party when it endorsed policies such as the abolition of the Saskatchewan Human Rights Commission. Saskatchewan Party also faced allegations of being the same old Conservative Party by another name.

Nevertheless, Saskatchewan voters unhappy with the NDP government were attracted to the Saskatchewan Party and in the 1999 election it nearly swept the popular vote in rural Saskatchewan. Popular vote, however, was not enough. The Saskatchewan Party failed to win enough seats to form the government.

With the Saskatchewan Party growing in popularity, it seemed likely they would defeat the NDP in the 2003 election. A platform advocating tougher immigrant rules, tax relief and privatized public transit, energy and utilities did not galvanize voters, however, and the party fell short. Hermanson stepped down as leader and Swift Current MLA Brad Wall assumed his role. Finally, in 2007, Wall succeeded the NDP to become the province's newest premier. Mr. Wall was reelected in 2011, winning 49 of 58 seats in the province.

THE CCF

The Co-operative Commonwealth Federation (CCF) was a socialist political party born during the Great Depression. Founded in Calgary in 1932, the CCF made its way to Saskatchewan in 1934.

During the CCF's formative years, Saskatchewan's United Farmers of Canada (UFA), and the provincial Independent Labour Party (ILP) merged as the leftist Farmer-Labour Party with a mandate to protect farmers against foreclosure, to socialize finance, and to establish a public health system. In 1934, the Farmer-Labour Party, whose ideas were similar to the CCF, joined the Saskatchewan branch of the CCF.

Initially the CCF had little success. Considered a radical socialist response to the crisis of the Great Depression, it failed to win public support in the 1934 and 1938 elections. By the 1940s, however, winds of change were blowing.

In 1941, Tommy Douglas assumed the leadership of the CCF and the CCF won in a landslide in the 1944 provincial election. With 47 of 52 seats, the Saskatchewan CCF became North America's first socialist government. Over the next two decades, the "radical" CCF proved it could work within the existing political structure as it engineered massive social and economic change. A hospital insurance program was followed by Medicare. Telephone and electric services were installed across the province and new high schools gave children unprecedented educational opportunity.

In 1961, Tommy Douglas resigned, replaced by Woodrow Lloyd. Under Lloyd, the CCF survived just one more term, going down to Liberal defeat in 1964. Nevertheless, the CCF had established a pattern of success for left-leaning politics. In 1971 and again in 1991, the New Democratic Party, a modern incarnation of the CCF, was elected to power.

Sources: Encyclopedia of Saskatchewan (On-line); Saskatchewan Council for Archives and Archivists.

Did you know...

that between 1944 and 1990, only 1.75 women were elected, on average, in each election in Saskatchewan?

Take 5 PREMIER BRAD WALL'S FIVE FAVOURITE THINGS ABOUT SASKATCHEWAN

Brad Wall was elected Premier of Saskatchewan on November 7, 2007. Hailed as "one of the best public speakers in Saskatchewan", Premier Wall was born and raised in Swift Current, where he still lives, along with his wife Tami, and their three children — Megan, Colter and Faith.

Premier Wall was first elected to the Legislature as the MLA for Swift Current in 1999. He was re-elected in 2003, became Leader of the Saskatchewan Party in March of 2004, and was elected Premier of Saskatchewan in the November 2007 provincial election.

1. **Potential for the future:** Saskatchewan has one third of the world's potash, roughly one third of the world's uranium and is Canada's second largest oil-producing province. This is a province with truly great potential. The goal for the future is to transform the current resource-driven boom into long-term prosperity for Saskatchewan families.

2. **Community spirit:** The people of Saskatchewan are more and more confident about today and tomorrow. They are increasingly self-assured but still humble, still very pragmatic.

3. **Quality of life/volunteerism:** Saskatchewan has one of the highest rates of volunteerism in the country. In communities all across our province, people spend many hours helping their neighbours on local boards and service clubs.

4. **Green spaces and parks:** There are tremendous tourism and recreational opportunities all across the province. Our regional and provincial parks have much to offer visitors and residents.

5. **Riders:** 2007 Grey Cup champions. A community-owned enterprise that exemplifies the Saskatchewan spirit.

They Said It

"You won't find me very interesting. I never do anything but work."

– Saskatchewan Premier, T.C. Douglas

PARTIES

Saskatchewan is home to eight registered political parties: the Green Party, the Heritage Party, the Liberal Party, the Marijuana Party, the New Democratic Party, the Progressive Conservative Party, the Saskatchewan Party and the Western Independence Party of Saskatchewan. The Liberals, Conservatives, the NDP and the NDP forerunner, the Co-operative Commonwealth Federation, have formed provincial governments. Currently, the provincial government is headed by the Saskatchewan Party with the NDP in opposition.

PREMIER PRIMER

- Number of Premiers who have served since 1905: 14
- First Saskatchewan Party Premier: Brad Wall
- First Liberal Premier: Walter Scott
- First Conservative Premier: James Anderson
- First CCF Premier: Tommy Douglas
- First NDP Premier: Allan Blakeney
- Youngest Premier: Charles Dunning, aged 36
- Longest-serving Premier: Tommy Douglas, 17 years
- Number of female Premiers: 0

Source: Online Learning Centre Saskatchewan

They Said It

"I have since been to Sicily. There I met the Mafia; when I told them I had worked for the Saskatchewan government, they were very much impressed."

– Graham Spry, nationalist and Agent General for Saskatchewan in the UK and Europe, 1947-48.

They Said It

"This is a job that you anguish over because you want to make sure that you're worthy of the confidence of your fellow citizens."
– Ray Hnatyshyn, upon accepting his position as Governor General.

THE CURRENT ADMINISTRATION

- Premier: Brad Wall, the 14th
- Party: Saskatchewan Party
- Number of seats won: 49
- Number of NDP seats won: 9
- Date of election: November 2011
- Voter turnout: 66 percent
- Saskatchewan Party's percentage of the poplar vote: 64.2
- NDP's percentage of the popular vote: 31.9
- Liberal's percentage of the popular vote: .06

THE CONSERVATIVE SCANDAL

In what was one of the biggest political scandals in Canadian history, 16 members of Grant Devine's Conservative government were convicted of fraud.

The controversy began in 1987 when Devine's caucus agreed to pool 25 percent of MLA's communications allowances into a central account. Allegedly, some members of the Devine government submitted invoices for services that were rendered – the problem was, these invoices went to bogus companies set up by John Scraba, Conservative caucus communications director. Once invoices were approved, cheques were issued to the phony companies and the money channeled back to several caucus members and Scraba.

Because of the scandal, the Saskatchewan Conservatives voted in 1997 to render their party inactive for the next two provincial elections to give it time to recover from the scandal. Devine has never been linked to the corruption.

Did you know...

that actor Kiefer Sutherland is the grandson of Tommy Douglas? Tommy's daughter, Shirley, married Donald Sutherland, Kiefer's dad.

FRANCHISE FACTS

- Year responsible government was implemented: 1897
- Year women earned franchise: 1916
- Year First Nations received federal and provincial vote: 1960
- Voting age: 18
- Residency: One must be a resident in the province for at least six months immediately before the date of the election writ.

Source: Elections Saskatchewan.

They Said It

"Early in my mandate, I challenged those advocating radical solutions for reforming health care — user fees, medical savings accounts, de-listing services, greater privatization, a parallel private system — to come forward with evidence that these approaches would improve and strengthen our health care system. The evidence has not been forthcoming."

– Roy Romanow, in his final report.

FEDERAL POLITICS

- Number of native born Saskatchewanians who have been Prime Minister: 0
- Number of voting districts: 14
- Members of Parliament: 14
- Number who are Conservative: 13
- Number who are Liberal: 1
- Senators: 6
- Number of Senators who are female: 3

Source: Parliament of Canada. 2011.

Take 5 FIVE MEMORABLE TOMMY DOUGLAS QUOTES

1. *"Canada is like an old cow. The West feeds it. Ontario and Quebec milk it. And you can well imagine what it's doing in the Maritimes."*

2. *"Courage, my friends; 'tis not too late to build a better world."*

3. *"I don't mind being a symbol but I don't want to become a monument. There are monuments all over the Parliament Buildings and I've seen what the pigeons do to them."*

4. *"Man can now fly in the air like a bird, swim under the ocean like a fish, he can burrow into the ground like a mole. Now if only he could walk the earth like a man, this would be paradise."*

5. *"The [Liberal] federal government's trouble is that they have a wishbone where they should have a backbone."*

Source: Brainy Quote; Thinkexist.com

PRIME MINISTER CONNECTION

Although no Canadian Prime Minister had been born in Saskatchewan, Prince Albert is the only Canadian constituency that has been represented by three Prime Ministers — William Lyon Mackenzie King, John Diefenbaker and Sir Wilfrid Laurier. In addition, Diefenbaker called Saskatchewan home in life and in death. At his death, his funeral train moved across the prairies until it reached its final stop – Saskatoon.

GOVERNOR GENERALS

Saskatchewan has connections with back-to-back Canadian Governor Generals. In 1984, Jeanne Sauvé, born in Prud'homme, was the first female to hold the post. Following her, Saskatoon lawyer and politician Ray Hnatyshyn became the 24th Governor-General serving from 1990 until 1995. His naming also marked a "first" in Canadian politics. Hnatyshyn was the first Ukrainian to be given the job.

Weblinks

Office of the Premier

www.gov.sk.ca/premier/

Featuring a biography, photos, press releases and contact information, this site is your link to the office of the premier.

The Legislative Assembly of Saskatchewan

www.legassembly.sk.ca/

Want to know what's going on in government? Check out this website that features a live webcam from the legislative chamber.

The websites, below, are maintained by the various political parties and provide information on their platforms, candidates and party events:

Green Party of Saskatchewan

www.greenpartysask.ca/

Saskatchewan Liberal Association

www.saskliberal.sk.ca/

Saskatchewan Marijuana Party

www.saskmp.ca/index.php

Saskatchewan New Democrats

www.saskndp.com/

Saskatchewan Party

www.saskparty.com/

Western Independence Party of Saskatchewan

www.wipsk.com

Then and Now

Now just over a century old, Saskatchewan is a relatively young province. This belies a much older heritage. With a past shaped as much by the First People as the newcomer farmer-settlers who came from around the globe, the history of the province of Saskatchewan is one of both hardship and success; most of all, it is about perseverance.

SASKATCHEWAN POPULATION, THEN AND NOW

1901	91,279
1921	757,510
1941	895,992
1961	925,181
1981	968,313
2001	978,933
2006	968,157
2010	1,038,018
2012	1,067,612

Sources: Statistics Canada; Encyclopedia of Saskatchewan; Government of Saskatchewan.

RURAL-URBAN DIVIDE

	Urban	Rural
1901	16	84
1921	29	71

1941	33	67
1961	43	57
1991	63	37
2011	64	36

POPULATION DENSITY, THEN AND NOW (PEOPLE/KM^2)

	Saskatchewan	Canada
1901	0.16	0.58
1951	1.46	1.52
2001	1.72	3.25
2012	1.75	3.75

Source: Statistics Canada; Government of Canada; Government of Saskatchewan.

THE PRAIRIE CHURCH

Often the first building erected in a new prairie community was the community church – a place where new immigrant neighbours could share language, culture, faith and camaraderie in their new prairie community. In first instances, they were modest log structures, but as money and materials became more available, they were often replaced by graceful buildings whose slim cross-marked spires or silver domes provided one of the only visible landmarks.

Many of these churches still dot the prairie landscape, though most face dwindling congregations and reduced schedules of services. Many of the churches are maintained by volunteer members who want to see the churches and their graveyards preserved as part of the legacy of so many of Saskatchewan's formative families.

Did you know...

that Cumberland House, first settled in 1774 as an HBC outpost, is the oldest continuously occupied settlement in Saskatchewan?

Take 5 BILL BRENNAN'S TOP FIVE PEOPLE
IN SASKATCHEWAN HISTORY

Bill Brennan teaches Western Canadian and Saskatchewan history at the University of Regina. He has written extensively about the history of Regina, and about Saskatchewan politics and government.

1. **Walter Scott.** As Saskatchewan's first Premier (1905-1916), his government built the handsome Legislative Building in Regina and created the University of Saskatchewan in Saskatoon. A farmer-owned elevator company (the Saskatchewan Co-operative Elevator Company) and a publicly owned telephone system (SaskTel) are also part of his legacy.

2. **"Tommy" Douglas.** Premier of Saskatchewan from 1944 to 1961, T.C. Douglas' greatest accomplishments were in the field of health care. Saskatchewan introduced Canada's first universal government-run hospital insurance plan in 1947 and its first universal Medicare scheme in 1962. While Douglas is often regarded as the "Father of Medicare," it was his successor, Woodrow S. Lloyd, who actually implemented Medicare over the strong objections of the province's doctors.

3. **Aaron Sapiro.** Having successfully organized farm commodity marketing pools in the United States, Sapiro played a key role in the creation of the Saskatchewan Wheat Pool. His whirlwind 1923 speaking tour of the province fired the imagination of thousands of farmers, and by 1924 the Pool was a reality.

4. **Ethel Catherwood.** Catherwood was born in North Dakota, but her family moved to Saskatoon in 1925. At the 1928 Olympic Games in Amsterdam the "Saskatoon Lily" won the gold medal in the women's high jump. She is still the only Canadian female athlete to win an individual gold medal in Olympic track and field.

5. **John Tootoosis.** Born on the Poundmaker Reserve, Tootoosis became a central figure in the creation of Saskatchewan's modern Aboriginal political organizations. After World War II he helped to create the Union of Saskatchewan Indians and its successor, the Federation of Saskatchewan Indians (now the Federation of Saskatchewan Indian Nations). He also deserves some of the credit for the entrenchment of Aboriginal rights in the 1982 Constitution Act.

They Said It

LIFE EXPECTANCY, THEN AND NOW

	Men	Women
1941	65.4	68.2
1961	70.3	75.9
1981	72.4	79.6
1996	75.4	81.3
2001	76.2	81.8
2012	77	82

NUMBER OF FARMS, THEN AND NOW

1901	13,445
1951	112,018
2001	50,598
2011	44,329

FARM WORKERS, THEN AND NOW

1901	31,772
1951	141,736
2001	51,525

Did you know...

that the Holy Trinity Anglican church at Stanley Mission is the oldest building in the province? Built between 1854 and 1860, it is made of local stone and timber and contains 10,000 pieces of stained glass.

FARM ACREAGE, THEN AND NOW (ACRES)

1901	3,833,000
1951	61,663,000
2001	64,904,000
2007	64,277,000

FARM INCOME, THEN AND NOW (TOTAL NET INCOME)

1926	$168,648,000
1951	$531,975,000
2001	$265,200,000

SCHOOL ENROLLMENT, THEN AND NOW (ELEMENTARY AND SECONDARY)

1900	24,000
1950	168,000
1970	247,000
1992	196,235
2004	174,263
2010	159,818

UNIVERSITY ENROLLMENT, THEN AND NOW

1920	647
1950	2,575
1970	14,069
2001	31,479
2005	32,838
2008	31,550

Source: Statistics Canada.

ALL THE LIVE LONG DAY

In the 1880s, the Canadian Pacific Railway (CPR) – aided by millions of federal dollars and millions of acres of land – became Canada's first national railway and the first to traverse the prairies. The CPR significantly influenced the development of western settlements.

Originally the CPR was to pass over the northern plains through such communities as Humboldt and Battleford en route to the Yellowhead Pass. Concerns about the encroachment of American railways into Canada, however, caused a change in plans and the CPR was moved south nearer the US border. This southern orientation forced the federal government to move the capital of the North-West Territories from Battleford to more southerly Regina in 1883.

Saskatchewan's railroads have been important to the province, providing much-needed transport to new settlers and key commodities, such as grain, and later, potash.

In recent years, reduced passenger service and cheaper means of transporting goods has led to the abandonment of rail service as grain and mineral transportation take to the road.

AUTOMOBILE REGISTRATIONS, THEN AND NOW

1906	22
1915	10,225
1925	77,940
1935	94,792
1945	140,257
1955	274,950

Did you know...

that while Saskatchewan had the fourth highest per capita income in Canada in 1928 at $478, by 1933 it was the poorest province with a per capita income of only $135?

Did you know...

that Francis Dickens, the fifth of 10 children born to famous British writer Charles Dickens and his wife Catherine, served with the North-West Mounted Police for 12 years and in 1883 was placed in charge of Fort Pitt?

1965	418,606
1975	613,269
2004	740,554

Take 5 SIGGA ARNASON'S FAVOURITE THINGS ABOUT GROWING UP IN SASKATCHEWAN

Sigga Arnason Springer grew up in the Holar postal district, was educated at Walhalla and Leslie, and attended the Holar Icelandic Lutheran Church. She and husband Bob Springer farmed for 25 years before moving into Foam Lake. Four of five children farm locally and a third generation will farm the family land. At 81, Sigga volunteers with the Solskin Icelandic Ladies Aid, Royal Purple, and other organizations.

1. **The people:** Saskatchewan people are known as volunteers. During World War II, Walhalla school organized a Junior Red Cross. It was just enough to know you have to share with those whose needs are bigger. We grew up during the Depression without knowing about the hardships. We had milk all year round and vegetables and beef. We used cardboard in our shoes when the soles wore out, but so did everyone. It isn't poverty when everyone is in the same boat.

2. **Clean air and the scenery:** We walked 3 miles to school, carrying our lunch, sandwiches in a jam pail and milk in a peanut butter jar, stopping along the way for a drink. No cups. I learned to love the sky during crisp star-filled December evenings.

3. **Christmas:** The school concert, with a "stage" platform, a wire to hold sheets that served as the stage curtain, and with crepe paper decorations. In the early years, there were real candles on the tree.

4. **Games and freedom:** When the new barn was built, we skipped on the smooth surface of the new concrete. We walked the six-inch planks that held up the beams, never realizing we could have fallen into the manger and broken our necks. We played scrub softball and Ante-Aye-Over.

5. **Opportunity:** In education, in agriculture – we have everything going for us. We boarded in Leslie for Grade 11 and 12. I wasn't interested in going, but a neighbour insisted that I carry on. I got married almost as soon as I finished.

They Said It

CAR CENTRAL

Detroit, Michigan is the famous home to the 'big three' automakers – Ford, General Motors and Chrysler. Less known is the fact that Saskatchewan was at one time the world's largest producer of cars.

In 1928, after the General Motors (GM) plant in Oshawa, Ontario had outgrown its capacity, the company set up shop in Regina. By mid-December, the first cars were rolling off the assembly line. Within a year, the Regina plant and its 800 employees were producing 30,000 cars a year. Saskatchewan seemed poised to become an automobile superpower.

As quickly as it began, Saskatchewan's car industry was gone. Initially it was sapped by the Great Depression. After a few months of struggle in 1930, the Regina plant closed. In 1937, as the recession eased, the plant reopened but with a workforce that had been halved, and workers could not meet the 125 car a day quota. The outbreak of war furthered the decline as Saskatchewan workers volunteered to serve overseas and as the plant itself was commandeered under federal law for the production of wartime goods. At war's end, General Motors was offered the return of its Regina plant. It turned the offer down.

Did you know...

that the SS Northcote, a steamboat that was first used by the HBC on the Saskatchewan River, holds the distinction of being the only warship to sail on the Prairies? It was called into service during the North-West Rebellion in 1885.

THE GREAT DEPRESSION

Saskatchewanians have taken many hits over the years, but none hit harder than the Great Depression of the 1930s. During the "Dirty Thirties," drought, grasshoppers and hail destroyed millions of acres of wheat, causing massive crop failures and turning the province into a dustbowl.

While all of Canada suffered through the Depression, agriculture-reliant Saskatchewan was the hardest hit. Net farm income dropped from $363 million in 1928 to just $11 million five years later. Farmers could simply not afford to go on and between 1931 and 1941, 250,000 people left the province.

REGINA RIOT

During the Great Depression, unemployed men found themselves in work camps toiling for 20 cents a day, meager meals, and a healthy dose of military-style discipline. By 1935, many were fed up with camp conditions and decided to travel to Ottawa and make their concerns known to federal officials.

On June 3rd, the men started their On-to-Ottawa Trek in Vancouver. By the time they arrived in Regina in mid June, they were 2,000 strong, and officials in Ottawa were getting antsy. Although the trekkers were peaceful, they were declared a social threat and police threatened to arrest them.

When the trekkers turned to the Saskatchewan government for help, the RCMP, aided by Regina city police, took matters into their own hands. Warrants were served on trek leaders at a peaceful Dominion Day rally. Violence erupted in downtown Regina and police fired into the crowd.

When the dust settled that July 1st, two men lay dead and hundreds were injured. The On-to-Ottawa trek was over, but Canadians were awakened to the awful reality of the Great Depression, especially for a generation of "lost" young men.

LET THERE BE LIGHT!

Well into the 20th century, electricity was a luxury not enjoyed by most rural Saskatchewanians. Electric power first arrived in 1890; by 1926, just 114 communities had power and they were served by an ineffective mishmash of small power companies. Most rural residents still depended on lanterns and woodstoves.

In 1929, this collection of power companies amalgamated into Saskatchewan Power Commission, but it would still be two decades before electricity became widespread. Indeed, by 1949, just 1,500 farms had power. That year, however, the Rural Electrification Act made Saskatchewan Power a crown corporation mandated with spreading the electric grid to the thousands of farms still not connected.

The task was daunting as farms in rural Saskatchewan were so isolated. In its first year, 1,200 farms were connected. By 1959, 40,800 were electrified and by 1966, 66,000 farms had power, along with hundreds of rural schools, churches and community halls.

CREDIT WHERE CREDIT IS DUE

Tommy Douglas is the "Father of Medicare." But a lesser-known resident of Saskatchewan named Matthew Anderson should be considered the Grandfather. More than two decades before the Douglas-inspired medicare plan was introduced in Saskatchewan, the settler introduced his own remarkable health care plan based on the system in place is his native Norway.

When he was elected a municipal councillor, Anderson lobbied for a universal health care system, fighting an uphill battle against reluctant politicians and physicians. In 1939, his lobbying paid off with the introduction of An Act Respecting Medical and Hospital Services for Municipalities. Unofficially, it was known as the Matt Anderson Plan.

The legislation gave residents in a given town the privilege of visiting or calling a doctor or hospital of their choice whenever they wanted. In return, residents over the age of 18 were subject to a personal tax of $5 per year, not to exceed $50 per family.

SASKATCHEWAN ROUGHRIDERS

In Saskatchewan, green is the colour and football is the game. Back in 1948, football was the game. But red and black were the colours.

The current incarnation of the Saskatchewan Roughriders began in 1910 as the Regina Rugby Club – rugby in this case being a sport that

Take 5 DR. STUART HOUSTON'S TOP FIVE SASKATCHEWAN HEALTH CARE FIRSTS

Stuart Houston – Order of Canada, SOM, DLitt, MD, FRCPC, and Professor Emeritus of Medical Imaging at the University of Saskatchewan – spent his entire medical career in Saskatchewan. An accomplished author, Houston has written eleven books and nearly 400 scientific papers and book chapters. His most recent book in medical history is *Steps On the Road to Medicare: Why Saskatchewan Led the Way*, published by McGill-Queen's University Press in 2002.

1. **1915:** Dr. Henry J. Schmitt, who worked in the rural municipality of Sarnia, was the first municipal doctor in North America.

2. **1929:** First province-wide universal, free diagnosis and treatment of tuberculosis.

3. **1946:** First comprehensive regional health care plan in Swift Current Health Region #1. This was two years ahead of Great Britain.

4. **1951:** First treatment of cancer with calibrated Cobalt-60 in the world. The first patient, with an apparently incurable disease, was cured and lived 47 more years!

5. **1962:** First province-wide medicare.

They Said It

resembled football more than rugby. In 1924, there was a move to give the team a catchier nickname. As luck would have it, another Canadian football team, the Ottawa Rough Riders had recently dropped their moniker in favour of the senators, and the Regina team quickly snapped "Roughriders" up. Then things got rather complicated when, just three years later, the Ottawa team reverted to its former name.

Still the name "Regina Roughriders" stuck and the red and black bedecked team had an amazing run. From 1919 to 1936, the team lost just six regular season games and boasted an amazing 11 undefeated seasons.

In 1948 the team was in for more changes. That year, teams in Moose Jaw and Saskatoon folded, and the Regina-based team became the provincial team – the Saskatchewan Roughriders. The team also underwent an image change, adopting its now beloved green and white colours. The origins of the team colours seem rather inauspicious. Chosen in an act of fiscal prudence, a team executive bought two sets of green and white jerseys that were on sale in Chicago.

While the Roughriders have only won the Grey Cup three times out of 16 championship appearances (the latest win coming in 2007, to the delight of fans everywhere) the "Rider Pride" of fans continues to endure as they cheer on their team through the highs and lows of each season.

Source: Back to the Past

Did you know...

that in 1956 four Roughriders players were killed in a plane crash as they were returning from an all-star game in Vancouver? The four players' uniforms are among the eight Roughriders numbers retired by the club.

GETTING AROUND

The coming of automobiles in the early 1900s revolutionized transportation in Saskatchewan, making travel and communication much easier especially for its many rural residents.

By 1906, 22 vehicles were registered in Saskatchewan. This grew to more than 10,000 by 1915 and to 60,000 by 1920, thanks to mass production, lower prices, safety and reliability improvements, and rising farm incomes.

The arrival of cars necessitated new roads and in 1955 a matrix of 19,000 kilometres of grid roads was introduced. For the first time, all settled areas of the province were connected with roads that could be used year round.

Today, Saskatchewan has the largest municipal grid road network in Canada. Combined with the province's highway network, Saskatchewan has more than 190,000 kilometres of rural roads – the most roads per capita in the world.

CROP INVENTION

Tall sun-ripened wheat swaying in the breeze has long typified the province's landscape. Today, seas of wheat share space with oceans of yellow – the dainty flowers of canola plants, Saskatchewan's new cash crop.

The story of Saskatchewan canola begins with Polish immigrants Fred and Olga Solovonuk who settled in Saskatchewan in 1928, bringing with them a handful of seeds of the rapeseed plant. Olga planted the original seeds in her garden on the family farm near Shellbrook. Each year she painstakingly harvested the plants' seeds, saving them until she had enough to plant a whole field.

Rapeseed proved valuable as a source of oil that made a fine industrial lubricant – something that came in handy during World War Two.

Did you know...

that Saskatchewan was the first province in the country to complete its stretch of the TransCanada Highway?

> "It is my firm belief that, if the government in office at that time, had amended the act, so the council of all municipalities in the province were duty bound to pass a bylaw giving the residents the opportunity to vote on the plan, we would have had complete medical and hospital care insurance for the whole province in the early 1940s."
>
> **– Medicare pioneer Matthew S. Anderson**

Rape oil, however, had a draw back – it was toxic to humans and live-stock and so had little use beyond industry. In the 1970s, Keith Downey and a team at the University of Saskatchewan bred a non-toxic rapeseed variety. The new seed was named Canola, derived from the words "Canada" and "oil."

When crushed, Canola seeds produce edible oil and a high protein solid which is fed to livestock. A quick glance at just about any food product label shows how popular the oil is. Low in saturated fat, it has become the oil of choice in many processed foods, from French fries, to margarine to baked goods.

Today the Canadian Canola business generates about $6 billion a year – a figure that would have been unfathomable to the modest Solovonuks! Canada remains the global centre for canola research and the crop is constantly being improved.

Did you know...

that Saskatchewan is home to one of the largest Icelandic communities in the world? The first Icelanders in Saskatchewan came to Churchbridge in 1885. Since then, they have kept their heritage alive. Many still celebrate Thorrablot, the Icelandic spring festival, Sumardagurrin fyrsti, the First Day of Summer, and enjoy Icelandic Independence Day picnics. In 1998, more than a century after the first Icelanders arrived, the Vatnabyggd Icelandic Club unveiled Saskatchewan's first monument to Icelandic pioneers at Elfros.

Weblinks

Saskatchewan Archives Board
www.saskarchives.com/
The Saskatchewan Archives was established in 1945 as a joint university-government agency. It has built one of the most comprehensive archival collections in Canada.

Saskatchewan Settlement Experience
www.sasksettlement.com/index.php
A part of Saskatchewan archives, this site contains the stories from before 1870 and up to the difficult Dirty Thirties.

Saskatchewan News Index
http://library2.usask.ca/sni/stories/index.html
This collection of Saskatchewan newspaper entries lets you examine, first hand, major events in the province's history.

Celebrating Saskatchewan's Heritage
http://olc.spsd.sk.ca/DE/saskatchewan100/index.html
This interactive website maintained by the Saskatchewan Western Development Museum is an amazing learning tool.

Northwest Resistance Digitized Project
http://library2.usask.ca/northwest/
Learn more about the North-West Rebellion with this site produced by Industry Canada.

The First People

IN THE BEGINNING

About 11,000 years ago, the glacier covering Saskatchewan slid north. By 6,000 years ago, it was gone, leaving behind a boreal forest, open woodland, aspen parkland and grasslands.

Before long, people lived there. Hunters followed the bison, wove fishing nets, built canoes, and developed trade routes along a river they called kisiskaciwanisipiy, meaning swift flowing river.

While the Egyptians were building pyramids, Saskatchewan's First People were meeting at Wanuskewin, setting up camps and then moving in pursuit of game. Each time they moved, they left behind evidence of themselves in their rock paintings, the petroglyphs at St. Victor and their discarded ceramic pots. They knew this land. It was home.

CREATION

Plains First People say that long before humans, cultural heroes were active on the earth. When a flood covered the earth, destroying all but aquatic creatures, three surviving aquatic animals – the beaver, otter and muskrat – were asked by these heroes to collect mud to use as building material.

Beaver tried first. Try as he might, however, he could not reach the bottom and bring up the mud. Then otter took up the challenge. He dove and dove, but each time surfaced empty handed. Finally, only muskrat was left. He was small and weak and the project seemed doomed. But muskrat had something special; he had courage and determination. On his last dive, he returned to the surface, exhausted, clutching precious mud in his tiny paw.

Hero blew on the mud and a small patch of land appeared. And then it grew. Hero shaped the landscape and replaced the drowned animals, but he still felt unfulfilled. Finally, he formed clay in his own image and breathed life into man and woman. Creation was now complete.

FIRST MEETING
The first European to travel to the Saskatchewan plains and meet its residents was Henry Kelsey. The HBC employee, who was seeking fur-trade partners, made the trek in 1690. Twenty five years later, another HBC employee, William Stewart, met the Chipewyan.

First Nations, who numbered 30,000 on the plains before the epidemics of the early nineteenth century took their toll, quickly became indispensable partners in the western fur trade. In 1730, the First People encountered something equally as important as HBC contacts; that decade the horse was introduced and began to revolutionize plains life.

ABORIGINAL AND EUROPEAN NAMES OF SASKATCHEWAN FIRST NATIONS
N'hiyawak – Plains Cree
N'hiyawak – Woodlands Cree
N'hinawak – Swampy Cree
Nahkawininiwak – Saulteaux
Nakota – Assiniboine
Dakota and Lakota – Sioux
Denesuline – Chipewyan or Dene

Bio PIHTOKAHANAPIWIYIN,

Pihtokahanapiwiyin, known as Poundmaker, has long appeared in Canadian history books as a rebel. Poundmaker, however, was no rebel. Even as his people starved, he counseled peace and his role in the uprising was misconstrued.

Pihtokahanapiwiyin was born in Saskatchewan. Part Assiniboine, part Métis, he was adopted on the death of his parents by Crowfoot, a leading Blackfoot chief. He earned the name Poundmaker as a young man because he displayed a keen ability in building bison pounds.

In 1876, during negotiations for Treaty 6, Poundmaker, then a minor chief, voiced concerns about dwindling bison herds and lobbied successfully for a famine provision in the treaty. In 1879, when the bison did disappear, Poundmaker looked to Ottawa to honour the treaty. Federal officials refused and Poundmaker and his people were forced to take reserve near Battleford.

Six years later, his community desperate, members of his band traveled to Battleford to lobby officials to honour treaty famine provisions. Poundmaker's men found the community empty – people had fled, afraid of the Métis insurgency – and helped themselves to food.

In response, Ottawa sent in troops. Displaying his trademark negotiation adeptness, Poundmaker managed to avoid major loss of life before he surrendered and was arrested at Batoche. Poundmaker was sentenced to three years in prison, falsely implicated in the uprising. He was released within three months but died shortly after. Chief Poundmaker was just 44 years-old.

They Said It

POPULATION

Métis and First Nations comprise 18 percent of Saskatchewan's population. The province's Aboriginal population is relatively young as half are under age 20, compared to the 26.5 percent of non-Aboriginals who are that young. It is projected that by 2045, 32.5 percent of Saskatchewan's population will be Aboriginal.

Total population   123,408

RESERVES

- There are 74 First Nation reserves in Saskatchewan. They cover 618,816 hectares (6188 km^2)— about 1 percent of Saskatchewan.
- Average reserve size in Canada: 176 hectares (1.8 km^2)
- In Saskatchewan: 4,313 hectares (43.3 km^2)

Source: Government of Saskatchewan.

URBAN RESERVES

Forty six percent of Saskatchewan's First Nations live on urban reserves, land located within a municipality or a Northern Administration District. Before a reserve is designated, the municipalities and First Nations negotiate fees for municipal services. Prince Albert, Saskatoon, North Battleford, Yorkton, Denare Beach, Duck Lake,Fort Qu'Appelle, Kinoosao, Kylemore, Lebret, Leoville, Meadow Lake, Pelican Narrows, Sandy Bay, Southend, Spiritwood and Sturgeon Landing are home to urban reserves.

Take 5 — SIMON MOCCASIN'S TOP FIVE REACTIONS AND CONSEQUENCES OF THE INFAMOUS "'60'S SCOOP"

Simon Moccasin is an, actor, writer, performance artist, comedian, teacher and also a Cree/Saulteaux/Blackfoot/Blood/Sioux and French. He loves to educate all on the importance of knowing one's culture and living it in a good way.

He explains, "I had the pleasure and displeasure of being ripped off of my reserve and made to live in a Westernized family. The program has become known as the 60's Scoop. Under the watchful eye of the federal government, the provincial government was hired to utilize their social services to go into reserves and scoop First Nations babies from their homes and put them into mostly Caucasian homes.

1. Loss of identity and culture and a sort of bi-polarness as the scooped awaken from their adopted dream and yearn for a sense of placement and belonging without knowing how to act in their original culture. With this comes two-way thinking which can also be a benefit, a bridge, if you will. I am a bridge, which is why it was also pleasurable.

2. Loyalty to the adopted family leads to forgetting and assimilating into Western Culture, forgetting about the sacred circle, the medicine wheel, the bison.

3. Fear and mistrust that comes from living in the westernized world, which is complete opposite of the Indigenous way of life. You are taught to fear everything and there is not much sense of faith and spirit.

4. The loss of spirituality — real spirituality that is carved out of all things beautiful in nature, and not some human made devices that help us to sleep some nights.

5. And, finally, the kinship ties are broken — if you want to break-up a culture forever, then break up the family unit.

SUN DANCE

The Sun Dance is an important Cree, Ojibwa and Blackfoot midsummer ceremony. The Sun Dance combines a ceremonial lodge, a sacred centre pole, abstinence from food and water, the fulfilling of vows and offerings to the sun. Ritual torture is also part of the ceremony as men attach themselves to the centre poll via a stick passed through the flesh of their chests. In a feat of strength and endurance, these men dance around the poll until the embedded stick pulls free. The ceremony is concluded with a feast. Although the ceremony was banned by the federal government from the 1880s until 1951, Sun Dances were held secretly and to this day the ceremony is conducted in a secluded setting.

SURVIVAL

The First People of Saskatchewan used their resources expertly. In the north, moose, elk and caribou provided food while hides were used in making clothing and tepee covers. On the plains, bison filled these needs. Because herds of large mammals were mobile, so were the First People. Ingeniously designed homes allowed women to disassemble them and move them as hunters pursued game.

Small game — geese, duck, fish, beaver and rabbit – spiced up the plains diet. As well, plants including wild rice and onions and berries supplement-

Did you know...

that of 74 First Nation Chiefs in Saskatchewan, thirteen are women?

Did you know...

that in 2005, the Dakota Dunes Golf Links, owned and operated by the Whitecap Dakota Nation, was named Canada's Best New Course by *Golf Digest*?

ed diets. Berries were also a central ingredient in the all-important staple, pemmican. This combination of dried berries and dried, powdered meat and fat kept well, was packed with nutrients, and was easy to carry.

First Woman

Member of the Peter Ballantyne Cree Nation, and from Deschambault Lake, in 2003 Joan Beatty became the first Aboriginal woman elected to the Saskatchewan Legislature and the first Aboriginal woman to be appointed to Cabinet.

She is one of 13 children and was raised in the traditions of the northern Cree. Her grandmother, Angelique Ballantyne, raised a family alone after losing two husbands and was a strong role model for Beatty. "She had no education. She trapped, and lived off the land," says Beatty. "She drowned a small moose by covering its eyes. She dyed roots to decorate birch bark baskets, used red willow and porcupine quills.

Beatty also says her grandmother was very strong in her faith, sang hymns by herself, and prayed every day. She didn't speak English, she says but no matter who came in from outside she was welcoming. "She was a wonderful example of being open. There was no racism with her."

Beatty herself was sent to Timber Bay residential school when she was 10. In the first year, she says she nearly lost her Cree. Students were not allowed to speak it, and Beatty was gone from September to June. "There's emotional loneliness in not being able to speak your language," she says.

High school required going south, to Glaslyn. It was her first experience with racism. "I was called a welfare kid. My dad paid for everything, so I was confused," she says. "You had to work doubly hard to prove yourself. People didn't accept you readily right away."

Beatty went on to become a journalist. She won the Best Documentary Award for her work on teen suicide. Beatty says there are particular challenges to being a First Nations provincial politician, but she says things are starting to turn around.

THE BISON HUNT

The Cree hunted bison year round, and moved in keeping with the rhythm of bison migration. The bison hunt varied by season. In summer, when the bison roamed the prairies, hunting parties would locate the animals, and hunters, mounted or on foot, would chase one bison at a time. Where possible, bison herds were corralled in a location where they were contained, such as a marsh, or they were run over a steep bank.

In winter, however, the giant mammals were trapped in pounds. The construction of pounds was supervised by shamans, whose spiritual powers would benefit the site. A circular area of 30 to 40 feet was cleared, and brush and logs assembled into a wall ten to fifteen feet tall. A runway was built leading up to the pound, making a sharp turn at the entrance to the pound. As bison approached, hunters on horseback would herd them into the pound, thus confining them for an easy kill.

LANGUAGE

Until the arrival of missionaries in the 1850s, Saskatchewan First People had no written language. Instead, they used stories and pictographs on rock, animal and vegetable dyes on animal hides and etching on birch bark to communicate and pass on their histories. Because Plains languages vary widely, the First Nations devised a standardized sign language which would allow easy communication from a distance.

Did you know...

that the Blackfoot call the meat of the bison "nitapiksisako," the real thing?

Bio BUFFY SAINTE-MARIE

Born in the Qu'Appelle Valley on the Piapot Cree Reserve in 1941, Buffy Sainte-Marie was adopted as an infant by an American family who raised her in the eastern USA. While she didn't spend her formative years on the prairies, the province has seen a lot of this famous Cree musician, artist and activist.

Sainte-Marie earned degrees in oriental philosophy and teaching and a doctorate in fine arts. Then she found success in songwriting. By the age of 24, her debut album, *It's My Way* won her *Billboard Magazine* praise as "Best New Artist." Her song "Until It's Time For You To Go," is just one of many recorded by such famous artists as Elvis Presley, Barbra Streisand and Roberta Flack. Sainte-Marie's Vietnam protest song "Universal Solider" became a peace anthem in the '60s, synonymous with the anti-Vietnam war movement.

Sainte-Marie became an icon to many, from Aboriginal communities to folk circles in Greenwich Village, to young fans of *Sesame Street* (where Sainte-Marie and her son Dakota Starblanket Wolfchild had a regular presence in the 1970s). By then, her First Nations activism was winning accolades, including the Louis T. Delgado Award for Native American Philanthropist of the Year.

In 1976, Sainte-Marie left the recording business to raise her son. But in 1983, she returned to music, recording *Coincidence* and *Likely Stories* and helping establish a Juno Award category for Aboriginal music.

She won an Academy Award for the song "Up Where We Belong," is a member of the Order of Canada (inducted in 1997), earned a space on Canada's Walk of Fame (1999), holds several honorary doctorates and has won the Lifetime Achievement Award from the Saskatchewan Recording Industry Association.

An educator before she found fame with her music, Sainte-Marie continues to educate students on a wide variety of topics including music and songwriting, Native American studies and women's issues.

LANGUAGE LITERACY (NUMBER OF FIRST NATION SPEAKERS, 2005)

English	95,100
Cree	20,000
Dene	5,100
French	1,600
Saulteaux (Ojibwa)	1,370
Dakota/Nakota/Lakota	140 or fewer
Mi'kmaq, Blackfoot, Dogrib	50 or fewer, combined

Sources: Victor Golla; Global Almanac 2005; Saskatchewan Indian Cultural Centre.

NUMBERED TREATIES

In 1870, the new nation of Canada bought Rupert's Land from the Hudson's Bay Company. Seeking to avoid the Indian Wars that plagued the USA, the Canadian government sought the peaceful transfer of land to settlers through treaties. First Nations were also keen to make a treaty – as bison disappeared and as European and American settlers inundated the west, they saw formal treaties as a way to protect their lands and futures. And so began a series of numbered treaties signed between the First People and the Canadian government; six were signed by First People of Saskatchewan.

Treaty 2: Negotiated in 1871, this territory covers a large section of Manitoba and a small portion of south-eastern Saskatchewan.

Did you know...

that the Pasqua Pictograph, returned to Pasqua First Nation on Aboriginal Day 2007, is the only known written record of a Treaty 4 signing from the perspective of the First Nations?

They Said It

Treaty 4: Negotiated in 1874, it includes southern Saskatchewan and was sought by First Nations who were starving in the face of the disappearance of the bison and other animals upon which they depended.

Treaty 5: Signed in 1875, it covers an area that is now mostly Manitoba, but includes a thin slice of mid-eastern Saskatchewan.

Treaty 6: Negotiated in 1876, it covers much of Alberta and the northern plains of Saskatchewan. The First Nations negotiators were only too aware of the impending loss of the bison and pushed hard for medical care and a provision for relief.

Treaty 8: This first northern treaty was signed in 1899 and covers 840,000 km^2 of northern B.C. and Alberta, the northwest corner of Saskatchewan and part of the Northwest Territories.

Treaty 10: This 1906 agreement covers northern Alberta and Saskatchewan. First Nations negotiators insisted on terms that included healthcare and education and the right to their traditional lifestyles.

Treaty making was rife with misunderstanding. For First Nations, the spoken context and oral promises of treaties was as important as the written texts. Government officials, however, believed the letter of the law lived on paper and oral promises were quickly forgotten. The two parties also understood the treaties differently. First People saw in the treaties a commitment to share the land. Government officials saw them as commitments to wholesale land surrender.

They Said It

RESIDENTIAL SCHOOLS

As life changed in 19th century Saskatchewan, First Nations recognized the value of European education and insisted that it be a treaty provision. The education they received, however, was not what they bargained for. Rather than a tool of advancement, schooling became a tool of assimilation and oppression.

Residential schools, joint church and federal ventures, were the most damaging; Saskatchewan was home to 22 such institutions. They separated children from their families and communities and insisted the surrender of Aboriginal culture, often subjecting students to abuse. The first such school was the Roman Catholic Qu'Appelle Industrial School, opened in Lebret in 1883. The last to close was Gordon Indian Residential School in Punnichy, whose doors closed in 1996.

Residential schooling has left a legacy of distrust and alienation. In a 1998 Statement of Reconciliation, the federal government acknowledged this painful legacy: "The Residential School system separated many children from their families and communities and prevented them from speaking their own languages and from learning about their heritage and cultures. In the worst cases, it left legacies of personal pain and distress that continue to reverberate in Aboriginal communities to this day."

Did you know...

that Saskatchewan-born Cree singer Buffy Sainte-Marie sang at NASA in 2002 to commemorate the space voyage of the first First Nation astronaut, John B. Herrington?

EDUCATION TODAY

Today Saskatchewan First Nations control their own educational destinies. The Saskatchewan Indian Community College, opened in 1976, now known as the Saskatchewan Indian Institute of Technologies, is one of Canada's original First Nation-controlled post-secondary schools.

The year 1976 also saw the creation of Gabriel Dumont Institute of Métis Studies and the Saskatchewan Indian Federated College. The latter is now the First Nations University of Canada and is North America's first accredited First Nations university.

Sources: Encyclopedia of Saskatchewan (book); Indian and Northern Affairs; Indian Resolution Schools Resolution Canada.

Weblinks

First Nations Bands of Saskatchewan

www.sicc.sk.ca/bands

Within these pages is information on the First Nation bands of the province of Saskatchewan. Information includes contact information, history, government, community and economic development, band programs and achievements, schools, annual events, tourist sites, and links.

First Nations and Métis Relations

www.fnmr.gov.sk.ca

The Department of First Nations and Métis Relations provides the Government of Saskatchewan with a more focused approach to its work involving First Nations.

Federation of Saskatchewan Indian Nations

www.fsin.com

This site represents 72 Saskatchewan First Nations, and aims to secure the protection and implementation of Treaties and Treaty Rights.

Go Ahead, Take Five More

As you can probably tell, we are partial to things you can count on one hand. This chapter is just more of that. It is designed to be fun, entertaining and insightful, not only in details about the city, but also about the person making the choices. It is a chapter that could have continued beyond the bounds of this book. Saskatchewanians, famous and not so famous, were literally bursting at the seams with opinions about their province.

TAKE 5: WAYNE MANTKYA'S TOP FIVE (OR SIX) MOMENTS IN REPORTING NEWS IN SASKATCHEWAN

For over 25 years, Wayne Mantyka has covered the stories that make the news in Regina and around southern Saskatchewan. Today, Mantyka reports on the happenings at the Saskatchewan Legislature for CTV, but throughout his career, he's had some great opportunities to help keep the public informed.

1. **Torrential downpour.** Hundreds of homes and businesses flooded during a severe rain storm in Regina lasting through the evening of June 25th, 1975. The water climbed so high as we drove the streets that we were forced to search for higher ground in a city that's virtually flat.

2. **Wild West.** Regina police went on a one day strike in May of 1976. Except for a few incidents of vandalism during the initial hours of the walkout, the city remained calm. It was the only day that motorists ran red lights if no traffic was coming.

3. **All the Buzz.** Apollo 11 astronaut Buzz Aldrin came to CKCK Television in 1975 for a live program. Aldrin was part of man's first walk on the moon. My career had only begun but I realized then that a greater interview opportunity could never occur.

4. **Faulty bus.** Reporters covering the 1978 Royal Visit of Queen Elizabeth traveled by police escort in a Saskatchewan Transportation Company bus. Reporters left events following the Queen's departure, yet we arrived at the next stop ahead of her in order to get the best photos. At the end of one trip, the driver of the media bus submitted an unusual fault report to STC mechanics, stating: "Coach won't exceed 90 miles per hour."

5. **Presidential visit.** Regina television crews like us were kept at a considerable distance as former U.S. President Bill Clinton left a Regina meeting in 2006. As he was about to enter his vehicle, he spotted a man wearing an early Clinton campaign t-shirt. Clinton couldn't resist walking over to ask where the shirt came from. By chance, the man was standing right next to us and we caught the exchange up close making for a great story!

TAKE 5: CHEF MOE MATHIEU'S TOP FIVE FAVOURITE DISHES

Moe Mathieu is the chef/owner of nationally-acclaimed Regina restaurant the Willow on Wascana, known for serving up Saskatchewan's best ingredients. Raised in Saskatchewan, Mathieu graduated with honors from the Culinary Institute of Canada, an experience he has combined with his roots to create delicious dishes.

1. Anything with Saskatoon berries including jam, sauce, pie, chocolates, in cream...

2. Perogies filled with almost everything we can think of including cheese, potatoes, sour cream, jam and meat sauce.

3. Bison steaks of all shapes and sizes with a big side of potatoes.

4. Cold northern lake pickerel pulled from the water, cleaned and pan seared in a cast iron pan with butter. Mmmm.

5. Turkey dinner with the fixings. Every family does it different but the spectacle of the family bird is one of our things for special occasions. If you can find Pine View Farms turkey, which is hormone free and free range, it is the best. Serve it with Saskatchewan low bush cranberry sauce.

TAKE 5: KEVIN HURSH'S TOP FIVE MOST IMPORTANT INNOVATIONS IN SASKATCHEWAN FARMING PRACTICES

Sometimes referred to as the voice of agriculture in Saskatchewan, Kevin Hursh is a consulting agrologist, freelance agricultural journalist, and broadcaster and farmer.

1. **The evolution and reduction of summerfallow:** In the early years of agriculture in the province, land was often cropped one year and left fallow the next. The practice of summerfallow has been dramatically reduced in recent decades and when land is left fallow, the weeds are usually controlled with herbicides rather than tillage. Saskatchewan is no longer a "dust bowl" on windy, dry years.

2. **Direct seeding:** Most of the crop in the province is now planted with zero or minimum tillage. The seeding and fertilizing operation is accomplished with one pass, often using seeding equipment designed and built within Saskatchewan.

3. **Cow wintering:** Saskatchewan has more cows than people and has the second largest herd in the country after Alberta. Increasingly, cow-calf producers are finding ways to let their cows forage and graze through much of the winter, thus decreasing the amount of feed that needs to be stockpiled.

4. **Crop diversity:** Long considered the wheat province, Saskatchewan has become a world leader in the production of many other crops including canola, durum, lentils, field peas, flaxseed, oats, canaryseed and mustard. Wheat acreage has steadily declined in favour of other more profitable cropping options.

5. **Intensive livestock operations:** Like other areas of the world, cattle and hog feeding is now done on a large scale. The greatest change has been in hogs. In the early 70s, there were tens of thousands of Saskatchewan producers raising a few hogs. Now there are only a few hundred producers, but the number of hogs raised in the province has never been larger.

TAKE 5: FOODIE AMY JO EHMAN'S TOP FIVE SASKATCHEWAN COOKBOOKS

Amy Jo Ehman is a writer and an advocate for local food in Saskatoon.

1. ***Arab Cooking on a Saskatchewan Homestead*** by Habeeb Salloum. Habeeb grew up on a hard-scrabble homestead near Swift Current after his parents emigrated from Syria. His cookbook is a collection of recipes and stories of how his mother served their favourite Arabic dishes right through the Dirty Thirties.

2. ***People and Places Cookbook*** by Bill Barry. Bill made a name for himself by tracing the history of place names in Saskatchewan. His cookbook continues that theme in photos, stories and recipes with names like Pile 'O Bones Ribs and Ituna Casserole.

3. *For the Breasts of Friends Cookbook* by the women of Foam Lake. It began as a community dinner to raise money for breast cancer research. Everyone asked for the recipes – and a cookbook was born. It was a national best-seller and now there's a sequel.

4. *The Hutterite Community Cookbook* by Sam Hofer. Sam grew up on a Hutterite colony and has written several cookbooks about their blend of old world German traditions with new world Saskatchewan ingredients.

5. *Fonos Fish Favorites* by Tara and Jonathon Fonos. The Fonos catch and sell fish – pike, pickerel, burbot and whitefish – out of northern lakes, so what better way to encourage more fish consumption than a cookbook with all their favourite fish recipes. Poor Man's lobster, anyone?

TAKE 5: LINDA MATTHEWS' FIVE FAVORITE FRUIT CROPS CULTIVATED IN SASKATCHEWAN

Linda Matthews is employed in the Fruit Breeding and Research Program at the University of Saskatchewan. She co-authored the book *Dwarf Sour Cherries: a Guide for Commercial Production*, so naturally her favorite fruit is sour cherries!

1. **Sour Cherry Fruit.** If you have eaten cherry pie then you have consumed sour cherry fruit. The fruit is typically used for processing and can be found in tins of cherry pie filling and most processed cherry products. Sour cherry cultivars released by the University of Saskatchewan are darker than the typical cultivar used in processing thereby eliminating the use of food dye or beet juice, which is added to current available products.

2. **Blue Honeysuckle Fruit.** I like to describe the shape of the fruit as an elongated blueberry and the flavour of the fruit as similar to blueberries. Blue honeysuckle fruit ripens in June. Rich in antioxidants, it

makes wonderful pie filling, ice cream, and preserves. The fruit is consumed in Japan where it is known as Haskap. Step aside blueberries, you now have a challenger!

3. **Saskatoon Fruit.** If you were born and raised in Saskatchewan then there is a likely chance that you have consumed saskatoon berry pie. This native fruit from the genus Amelanchier has a long tradition of use dating back to native peoples. The round, purple fruit ripens in July and is commonly used to make pies, jam, jelly and syrup. To the newcomers of Saskatchewan, "refine your palette and enjoy the flavour experience that saskatoon fruit has to offer."

4. **Chokecherry Fruit.** Another native species commonly marketed as the "wild black cherry" to appease wary consumers, this astringent fruit makes excellent jelly and syrup. Products made from chokecherry fruit are an intense red colour with a unique tart flavour.

5. **Strawberry Fruit.** Strawberries grown in Saskatchewan are red, juicy and flavourful. The fruit is nothing like the firm and flavourless imported fruit that seduces us with its wonderful red colour, which is available at local grocery stores in late winter. Be patient, Saskatchewan residents. Local pick-your-own strawberry farms open in July. It is worth the wait!

TAKE 5: NOELLE CHORNEY'S FIVE FAVOURITE PATIOS IN SASKATCHEWAN

Chorney is a Saskatoon-based writer whose passion is food — eating it, growing it, cooking it and matching drinks to it. While she writes about everything from gardening to plasma physics, she is best known for her regular dining column in *Planet S*, Saskatoon's City Magazine.

1. **Amigo's Cantina (Saskatoon):** Tucked away in the back of this bustling live music venue with fresh, Mexican-inspired dining is a quiet patio, shaded by a large elm tree, protected from the alley by a tall fence, and brightened by a bright orange wall. The overall effect is quiet and cozy – the perfect place to while away a summer afternoon, sampling a bean and olive burrito or monster plate of Nachos Grande and sipping on your favourite brew.

2. **La Bodega (Regina):** I first visited La Bodega for its excellent food and impressive cocktail list. But I soon discovered not one but three patio options – dine al fresco on the stone patio just outside the building and protected from the street by a tall fence, on a smaller wooden deck off the bar, or head to the rooftop, past pot herbs that will likely make it into your meal, for another fresh-air option.

3. **O'Shea's (Saskatoon):** I'm a sucker for rooftop patios in general, and I couldn't decide whether to mention O'Shea's pub or the Yard and Flagon on Broadway (this is my way of trying to make a top 5 list really a list of six places). O'Shea's won out because it holds more people (although it's still usually packed), and there's a staffed bar right on the patio for quicker service (the burgers and shepherd's pie are good too).

4. **Zest (Regina):** A little gem housed in the Saskatchewan Science Centre offering gorgeous, local food inspired by international flavours (think curry-rubbed bison or ancho-espresso pork) and a peaceful view of Wascana Park from its welcoming cobblestone patio.

5. **Spadina Freehouse (Saskatoon):** With the best up-close view of Saskatoon's "castle," the Delta Bessborough, and Kiwanis Memorial Park, the Spadina Freehouse's cobblestone patio places diners front and center in Saskatoon's summertime action by the river. While people-watching, enjoy creative cocktails or a selection from the robust beer and wine list, all great matches to ever-changing pizza, sandwiches, entrees, or my favourite snack, the sweet potato fries.

TAKE 5: GERRY KLEIN'S TOP FIVE SASKATCHEWAN INNOVATIONS

Gerry Klein is a columnist and editorial writer for *The StarPhoenix* and was formally the paper's University Editor. Innovation is, by its nature, our species' ability to stand on the shoulders of our ancestors, and build on their ideas. It is the hallmark of Saskatchewan.

1. In 1907, the government of Saskatchewan passed the University Act, establishing the University of Saskatchewan (U of S). It was a unique institution not only in that it grouped together on one campus colleges of agriculture and arts and sciences but also had a board of governors completely independent from its political masters, allowing it to set the research and teaching agenda needed to help the province become, within a generation, the third largest in the country. The university went on to have the greatest selection of life sciences collected on one campus of any English Canadian university.

2. In 1892, an agricultural researcher based in Ontario, named Percy Saunders, took samples of Red Fife wheat that were grown in Saskatchewan, and crossed them with an early-ripening variety of wheat from India called Hard Red Calcutta. The result was Marquis wheat—a variety with large yields that matured 20 days earlier than common varieties. This new wheat was later shipped to Indian Head for further testing. In 1911, Rosthern farmer Seager Wheeler made the grain famous when he won a prize of $1,000 in gold coins for "the best hard spring wheat grown in North America."

3. In 1933, U of S President Walter Murray, desperate to save money during the depression asked single faculty members to take a sabbatical with just three months pay. Chemistry professor John Spinks used this time to study with Gerhard Herzberg in Darmstadt, Germany. When Hitler passed the notorious Nuremberg Laws, banning Germans from marrying Jews, Herzberg left his homeland and found a home, with Spinks, in Saskatoon.

Herzberg, who would go on to win the Nobel Prize, attracted such a strong cadre of physicists to the U of S that the university led the world in such fields as atmospheric studies, particle science and medical radiation.

4. In 1962, the Medical Care Insurance Act, passed by Saskatchewan CCF government, is the first comprehensive public-health system in North America. Former Prime Minister John Diefenbaker asked Supreme Court Justice Emmett Hall (both from Saskatchewan) to prepare a White Paper on a national health care system. It is from that paper Canada's current system sprung.

5. In 2004, the Canadian Light Source officially opened on the U of S campus. This $173.5-million behemoth is the most powerful research facility in Canada, which uses synchrotron light to study the molecular structure of matter. It is the ultimate tool for standing on our ancestors' shoulders, allowing scientists unequaled opportunities to advance studies in everything from engineering to plant science to geology to health care.

TAKE 5: DEREK TURNER'S TOP FIVE THINGS TO DO FOR FREE IN SASKATCHEWAN.

Derek Turner is a freelance writer and aspiring teacher from Saskatoon, Saskatchewan. As a university student in both Saskatoon and Regina, he spent a lot of time finding ways to spend his time that did not involve spending money. His weblog is located at derekbturner.blogspot.com.

1. **Go for a walk along the Meewasin Trail in Saskatoon.** The trail provides an amazing view of the city's landmarks as it runs along the South Saskatchewan River, passing by reminders of the city's early years. The River Landing development is transforming the southern portion of the trail, and should continue to improve Saskatoon's downtown core in years to come.

2. **Window shop** along 13th Avenue in Regina, Broadway Avenue in Saskatoon, or in downtown Saskatoon. These are all home to unusual shops and markets whose owners and proprietors are typically more interesting than their merchandise.

3. **Tour a small town and soak in the culture of a place.** Many towns have a museum or cultural centre with free information and help for tourists. War memorials, cemeteries and historical sites offer additional information about the town and surrounding area, and older residents – often found at the local coffee shop – are almost always eager to share stories of the town's past with interested listeners.

4. **Volunteer.** Saskatchewan has hosted many world-class events in recent years, including the Juno Awards, World Junior Hockey Championships, Vanier Cup, and Grey Cup. Participants, spectators, and residents often credit the spirit of the people of Saskatchewan as the key to the success of these ventures, as well as regular events such as WHL games, theatre performances, and annual fundraisers like Telemiracle.

5. **Watch a sunset.** Saskatchewan is called "Land of Living Skies" for good reason. In the heart of summer, it is possible to spend up to two hours watching the oranges, reds, and yellows of the setting sun weave an arresting tapestry on the horizon.